Andy,
Thank you for y[...]
on Rotary Club board 2019/20
Kathleen

COURAGE in the
FACE of CRUELTY

MY TWENTY-EIGHT YEAR
JOURNEY THROUGH THE
CALIFORNIA PRISON SYSTEM

Encouraged by your presence!
James Alexander

Praise for
Courage in the Face of Cruelty

"If you want to know about our painful prison system, both the heartbreak and the redemption that is possible, James tells the truth in his vivid, moving story."
—*Jack Kornfield, bestselling author and founder of Spirit Rock Center, Woodacre, California*

"I truly believe that James Alexander is the Nelson Mandela of America. He has met a multitude of challenges, including 28 years of incarceration in our much-maligned prison system, and has emerged as an object lesson in redemption and a teacher to all people. The book is a no-holds-barred account of a man on his way to greatness."
—*Richard Grace, author, vintner and philanthropist*

"James Alexander spent every minute of the 28 years he served in the nation's toughest prisons for an accidental murder refining and purifying himself until virtually everyone he came in contact with recognized him as a special being. Everyone. Including his guards and parole board, which three times recommended him for parole only to be countermanded each time by Governor Schwarzenegger. The courts eventually overruled the governor. James left prison as one of the kindest, most spiritually developed men I have ever met, and that includes His Holiness, the Dalai Lama. Read his inspiring book and learn what an attention fixed on compassion and helping others can generate in the midst of Hell, and what 'real' toughness looks like."
—*Peter Coyote, Zen Buddhist priest, actor and author*

COURAGE in the FACE of CRUELTY

MY TWENTY-EIGHT YEAR JOURNEY THROUGH THE CALIFORNIA PRISON SYSTEM

JAMES ALEXANDER

LONELY MONK PRESS

Walnut Creek, California

Lonely Monk Press
1966 Tice Valley Blvd. #270
Walnut Creek, CA, 94595
jamesalexandercourage@gmail.com
jamesalexandercourage.com

Book layout conceptualized by Allyson Edwards
Interior Layout by Ruth Schwartz, thewonderlady.com
Cover and author photos by Briana Marie Photography

About the cover: His Holiness, the Dalai Lama, who is the cultural leader of Tibet, honored James Alexander in 2014 as an Unsung Hero of Compassion for his work helping to develop groups in prison to benefit inmates.

Ordering Information:
Quantity sales. Special discounts are available on quantity purchases by corporations, associations, and others. For details, contact the "Special Sales Department" at the address above.

COURAGE in the FACE of CRUELTY: My Twenty-Eight Year Journey Through the California Prison System / James Alexander—1st ed.
ISBN 978-1-7331537-0-6 paperback
ISBN 978-1-7331537-1-3 ebook
Library of Congress Control Number 2019907609

Dedication

To my beloved mother, Gloria, whose perseverance in enduring much hardship instilled in me the attitude of never giving up.

To my supportive aunt, Sybil Alexander, whose life of service as a union organizer, social rights advocate—and with her feisty New Yorker personality—showed me the necessity of speaking truth to power.

To my wife, the wonderful Constancia Alexander, whose tenderness showed me that even after 28 years of prison it was still possible for me to enjoy intimacy and the fulfillment of a loving relationship.

Acknowledgements

To the people who helped bring this book to life:

Dr. Sol Weingarten, who has greatly helped me in bringing this book into fruition. I thank him for his encouragement in recognizing that I have the fine qualities of character that can be used as a model to bring about effective transformation of the prison system and its inmates with the publication of this book. His invaluable insights continue to be a beacon on my continued journey through life.

Allyson Edwards, for her amazing efforts and steadfast assistance with research and organization in ensuring that this book is as accurate as possible. I also appreciate her wonderful attitude in always being positive and willing to help.

Karen Villandre, for her balanced efforts to provide sensible advice in the furtherance of the goal of bringing a worthwhile book into existence, which could effectively shine light onto our prison system.

Lynn Braxton, Terry Bisson, and Matthew Gilbert, for their dedicated and effective editing to make the content of the book flow for the reader.

Ruth Schwartz, for her technical expertise in bringing this important book to publication.

To the friends and family who supported my efforts to fight for freedom in prison:

Gene Kirkham. Without his courage and compassion, my freedom could quite possibly still be in doubt.

Gene's family, for opening their home and heart to me.

Cody Gillette-Kirkham, for sacrificing her weekends to visit me in prison, and upon my release, introducing me back to nature.

My brother, Ronald, and his family.

My brother, Robert, and his family.

My sister, Lynn, and her family.

John Kelly, for his spiritual advice and always standing by me.

Pat Tubman, for visiting me and supporting my educational goals that I achieved while in prison.

The community of KAIROS, for their continued dedication of bringing light to those incarcerated in California prisons.

The community of the Alternatives to Violence Project, for their general activity of going into prisons across the United States of America to deliver beneficial help to one of the most sorely needy populations.

To all in my Quaker community, for always holding me in the light.

To the many others who continue to be supportive of me on my journey:

To my fellow Marines: Semper Fidelis.

Dick Grace's men's group in Saint Helena, California.

The Sonoma County Department of Health Services, for enabling me to work with groups of individuals who committed the serious offense of drunk driving and are in need of help to prevent recidivism.

The people of Saint Helena, California, for providing a most welcoming atmosphere for my re-entry into society.

My Chicago family.

The many prisoner friends that I benefited from having in my life at its most difficult period.

The correctional officers who were fair-minded and supportive of prisoners in these most difficult prisons.

Special thanks to Betsy Crites, Eric and Erica Sklar, Liz Tregaskis, Dan Lambert, Dr. Tom and Mary Dixon, Bill and Tess Hagemann, Ellen Eggers, Alice Waco, Alex and Sonya Perrotti, Kim Richards, Peter Tracy and Marcia Ford, William Simon, Ann Boone, David and Sharon Beckman, Jim Avera and Barbara Babin, Barbara Flynn, Derrick West, Tony Holzhauer, Kyle Woolum, Kay Davis-Bissonett, John McKinney, and Gary Thornton.

To the many other human beings who have assisted me on my journey. Please forgive me for not mentioning you by name. Let there be no doubt—all of you have a place in my heart. I am, and will always be, encouraged by your presence.

Table of Contents

Chapter One

In the Beginning

The cell was dark and musty with all the grimness of the thousand poor souls who had slept there before me. It was my first day in solitary confinement at San Quentin's "maximum security administrative segregation unit," commonly referred to as "the hole." The majority of inmates there had been sentenced to die; for the few like me not on Death Row, the message was clear: play by the rules or else—if you managed to stay alive long enough to learn them.

I was sent there for stabbing another inmate while attempting to survive the "gladiator school" of Soledad prison where I'd been placed in 1985, two years after being convicted of second-degree murder stemming from an unintentional homicide. Soledad had earned the "gladiator" rep because many of its inmates were young, newly incarcerated, and eager to make a name for themselves, usually through violence. Many of the staff there seemed to relish their authoritative role in that violent and chaotic environment. The guards believed that if inmates could be turned against each other, they wouldn't have the time or inclination to focus their anger on them. The warden, realizing he couldn't control the guards, imposed the harshest discipline he was allowed to under the law on inmates who got out of line. When I placed myself in a situation to strike back against another inmate who had attacked me, the warden condemned me to the worst nightmare in the entire California prison system—the hole in San Quentin.

My twenty-fourth birthday had not yet arrived. I had spent three years in the Marine Corps and felt I could handle any situation. Now, I wasn't so sure. In that cold, dark, damp cell, I wondered how things had become so bad and if I'd survive the consequences. Is this what my life had come to before having fully lived it? Would this be the end of my journey?

I grew up in the Chicago housing projects. My most vivid memory of those early years was waking up in the early morning and watching my mother get ready for work, leave the apartment, and walk down a long narrow hallway past an elevator that never seemed to work. The stairwell was always filthy and rank with the smell of urine. The railings and steps were sticky with human squalor. Some days an addict would be lurking in the dark, desperate for money to finance his next fix. I remember being constantly frightened that something bad would happen to my mother. Some people dealt with the fear by shutting down, but because my mother's safety was so important to me, it pushed me to be tough and smart in whatever way I could.

I decided to get to know some of these guys who made their living on the streets. I figured that if anything happened to my mother, they would probably have a good idea who did it. I began by pitching pennies with them, which soon became nickels, then dimes and quarters. Pitching pennies is a game of gambling where individuals toss a penny towards a designated line on the sidewalk. The object of the game is to get your penny on the line or as close as possible to that line. At first, they harassed me for being so young, but I kept showing up and they finally got used to me. I also got pretty good at pitching because I was short in height and could contort my body low to the ground, which took away a lot of those unpredictable bounces. I learned I could toss the coin even better and more consistently when I controlled my breathing. I got so good that a crowd would form just to watch me pitch coins. The "street guys"—the pimps, gangsters, and hustlers who ruled my "hood"—were just as impressed. As they got to know me, they got to know my mother and would actually speak to her when she got off the bus and walked toward our apartment building. They showed her a great deal of respect, and I was proud that I'd found a way to protect her.

My mother always wanted something better for her kids than what she received growing up, and I tried to honor that; but she used to chide my optimism by saying, "You must think we're rich!" She couldn't figure out where my confidence came from because "Money don't grow on trees." It surely did not, but I found myself wondering how the street guys were able to have so much money.

Like a lot of young black kids, I was fascinated by the pimps and the way they carried themselves. Each one could be identified by his cars, his women, his facial hair, and especially by his signature colors. When a certain color of car pulled up, you knew immediately who would step out of it.

Each pimp took great pride in his public appearance and would spend whatever was necessary to project an image of prosperity. One in particular—let's call him Don—loved the colors green and gold. Everything he owned, including his many vehicles, had to be green and gold. It was his trademark look and my first real education in brand marketing. I used to take the bus to visit my friend Steve who lived in one of the better neighborhoods. His father owned a restaurant and Don would always show up there on Tuesday afternoons. It was an event. Steve and I would watch for him to drive up in one of his green-and-gold cars. Some days it was the Rolls, some days the Cadillac, and some days the customized van. The Lincoln Continential, which we called the "stretch-me-out limo," was our favorite.

One day I got the courage to ask Don if we could wash his van, which had images on the sides of nearly naked women in green and gold lingerie. He'd seen us hanging around and probably knew that Steve's father owned the restaurant, so maybe that's why he gave us the nod. Steve and I rushed to get a bucket and some rags and turned on the hose. After we had the van looking shiny, I said, "Steve, let's get in."

"Hell no!" he said, shaking his head as I opened the door and looked inside. I saw wall-to-wall fake fur, long velvety cushions, and a small refrigerator. I reached in and stroked the fur, amazed at how good it felt. I was about to climb inside when I heard—a silence—behind me. I turned, and he was standing right there. Don. I looked at him and, in one quick breath, asked if he wanted us to clean the inside too.

"Next time, lil' man," he said as he handed each of us a crisp new five-dollar bill. Some people think pimps are all about sex, but they're really all about money.

The so-called gangsters had their own distinct ambitions. They were concerned with more than just money and color-coordinated fashion; they wanted power. Like a lion in the jungle lording over its pride, each leader wanted the biggest gang in the neighborhood and each went about it in one of three ways: The charismatic leader attracted followers who wanted to be in his presence. The aggressive leader commanded through fear. Although his methods were effective in the short run, he cared little for long-term loyalty and followers would usually figure out how to remove him. Somewhere between the charismatic and aggressive leader was the tactician, the one I became most intrigued with. Like a chess player puzzling out multiple possible moves and scenarios, the tactician understands that there are many ways to get to Rome. He doesn't make friends and easily creates enemies, ruling by fear, charisma, and cunning. He is ultimately heartless in how he treats people but gives the appearance of caring deeply for their well-being. No one can get close to him, not even his own mother. He is ruthless with his enemies, especially in public. Tacticians are driven by fantasies of world domination. They dream of an epic death, an exit talked about decades later. Full of pride and ego, their conversation is grandiose and their actions over the top. The tactician is the worst and best type of gangster. And usually very successful.

Then there were the hustlers. They had little pride or ego. They didn't care how they looked, dressing only for whatever a particular hustle required. They didn't like gangs or groups. They were resourceful and independent, experts at panhandling, picking pockets, and sometimes outright robbery. Hustlers always had money, though it often looked like they didn't. When their funds got low, they'd just work the streets until they got the cushion they needed. A true hustler almost never gives up. Other than money, the only thing that moves a true hustler is a better hustle.

The streets in Chicago were owned by pimps, gangsters, and hustlers; many of the kids in the projects chose one of those three career paths. But it was tough to become a pimp because that took a certain skill set, and the same was true with becoming a hustler. Both required a temperament and a chutzpah that most kids didn't have. So, in Chicago's inner city, many children of the streets joined a gang. Despite their vicious tactics, gangs offered a form of camaraderie and belonging. It does seem as though human beings have a need to join something and feel connected. Gangs provided those bonds no matter how misdirected their goals. Each member was given a position within the hierarchy and kept in line by a distorted kind of discipline. With so many broken families it was better than the alternatives, but a hard way to feel connected. I wasn't looking for any of that, though; I only wanted money to take care of me and my family. And since I wasn't willing or able to follow the steps of a hustler or a pimp, I chose a fourth path: excelling at school and working a normal job.

At school, I did well because I was motivated to learn as much as I could. And though I wasn't the oldest, I was in charge of getting my brothers up, fed, and off to school. I was the middle son and I guess my mother felt she could count on me to be responsible. So, I made sure things were ready in the morning and the apartment was locked when me and my brothers left for school. I was still very young, maybe nine or so. My older brother was two years older and my younger brother was three years younger. I would wake up at the same time as my mother, help with breakfast, and watch her walk out of the apartment.

I delivered newspapers in the early morning and found other jobs such as shoveling snow for neighbors or bagging groceries at the local store. I was learning a lot about responsibility. On the way back from school, I would always stop at the store to buy chocolate milk and junk food. It began as a way of rewarding myself for doing well, however, it became a behavioral pattern of unhealthy eating. I felt proud because I could afford to buy whatever kind of junk food I desired.

As a result, I gained a lot of weight and was often teased for being chubby. My self-esteem suffered greatly and I didn't have many friends. But I really liked studying and getting good grades, so when it came to my intellect, I was confident in myself and found a great deal of solace in enhancing my knowledge. I was especially good in math; I studied hard and my teachers noticed. They tested me and found I had an above-average IQ—the kind of kid who had a chance for college.

An opportunity came up for a handful of kids in my eighth-grade class to attend one of the best public high schools in Chicago—Lane Technical. It was located on the city's north side and was way ahead of closer schools in its quality of teaching and coursework. Because I was an outstanding student, I was chosen to go, along with two others. The three of us would travel by bus from where we lived on the deep southwest side, a trip that took an hour and a half. We took one bus east that dropped us off on a bare corner where we would wait for the next bus heading north. We would meet other kids making their way to Lane on that same corner. In winter, which hits Chicago hard, the wait was almost unbearable. There was nothing to block the wind from tearing through our coats. We would huddle together to stay warm. We became very close, and even today we still stay in contact.

My class was small but had the smartest and coolest black kids in the mostly white school, where blacks made up only seven percent of the student body. Most schools in Chicago were still segregated at the time. The Supreme Court case Brown v. Board of Education had been decided decades earlier but the wheels of justice, especially when race is involved, move more slowly than molasses on a cold stack of pancakes. So even in 1976, more than twenty years after that monumental legal decision, many schools were still primarily segregated. More relevant to me, though, was that while I excelled academically, my social life was anything but fulfilling. I was still overweight, shy even among my black classmates, and not very popular.

After school, I worked at a used car dealership a few blocks from where the Chicago Cubs played their baseball games and then went straight home. Working at that dealership turned out to be a useful lesson in business. I'd watch a customer come in and say they were just looking. The salesman would respond, "Of course. I'll leave you alone to look around. Let me know if I can help you with anything." Then he waited like a tiger eyeing its prey. At the exact moment when the customer would pause at a car that caught his eye, the salesman would show up to open the door, take them for a test drive, and tell them what a perfect fit this model was for them. I wanted to learn how to do this but being only fifteen, I was put to work as a stock boy in the parts department. I showed up every day, ready for work, and it seemed that everyone at the dealership liked me. I became so engrossed with the job that I found myself thinking of little else. I saw a new career path emerging—the used car business!

When I wasn't at school or work, I'd be eating, studying, or sleeping. I didn't get invited to many parties and was content to be left alone with my junk food. I did help a couple of the more popular kids with their homework, which put a few extra dollars in my pocket to subsidize my food habit, and to buy clothes and some things for our apartment. My mother was proud of the way I was applying myself and grateful that I hadn't chosen the life of a pimp, gangster, or hustler. I was earning my own money and doing it legally.

My father lived elsewhere and was not a constant part of my life; I thought it was because he was ashamed of how chubby I was. He left us (me, my mom, and my older brother) when I was three and didn't come back into my life until I was eleven. During that time, my mother found intimacy with another man and my younger brother was born. Seven years after that, my mother met and married another man and my little sister was born. I was ten years old when my little sister was born, and her father became my last stepfather, but I always loved and admired my father.

My dad was strong and healthy, worked hard, and didn't mind spending money on me and my brother. He would take us to mom-and-pop restaurants where he'd order us grits and eggs with toast and sausage or bacon. I remember once being scolded by my father for putting sugar on my grits. I didn't understand the significance of this until years later. He was born in Arkansas. Black men born in the South in the 1940s were considered "country boys," and you'd never find a true country boy putting sugar on his grits. That was for city or "sissy" boys. Country boys used salt, pepper, and butter, and, my father wouldn't tolerate any sissy boys in his family. He also spent considerable time trying to slenderize me by any means possible, ordering me to do sit-ups when I got up in the morning and then again before I went to bed—twice a day and still I didn't lose weight. He wanted me to be strong and tough, and I did everything I could to fit that image and make him proud of me, but nothing worked.

Two years into high school, life hadn't changed much. I was still feeling lonely, spending most of my time eating and working. One of my regular homework clients was a popular white kid on the football team. He was very athletic, very cool, and he came from a two-parent, middle-class family. Everybody wanted to hang out with him. He decided to give a party that promised to be the biggest of the school year. Anyone who was anyone at Lane would be there. Since I was dealing with my self-esteem issues, I hadn't really thought about it, and most of the kids who would be there didn't know me anyway. You can imagine my surprise, then, when this admired athlete stopped me in the hallway and invited me to his party. He must have felt that I'd really helped him get through his classes. I told him I'd definitely be there. I can still remember standing in that hallway in shock asking myself again and again if he really did invite me. I was smiling all the way home on both buses.

When I got to our apartment, the first thing I did was run to the kitchen and ask my mother if I could go. She asked me where the party would be and when it would start. I told her it was on the other side of town at the home of one of the white kids who went to the school and that it would start about seven o'clock. She shook her head. "That's too far to travel for a party, James," she said firmly. "It will be dark before it even starts, and you're only sixteen." I was devastated. The one opportunity I had to finally, legitimately mingle with the cool kids at Lane was being denied. So, I made a decision to defy my mother.

The night of the party I put on my cleanest shirt, the coolest pair of pants I had, and a pair of Stacy Adams shoes that shined so much you could have used them as a mirror. The final touch was a new black leather coat my father had just given me for my birthday. Though he didn't live with us, I still felt very close to him, so that coat was precious to me.

As soon as my mother settled into her television chair, with her back to the door, I made my escape. It was the dead of winter but as I waited in the cold and dark for the elevated train, my excitement kept me warm. I was imagining how the night would turn out: strolling through the door, everyone turning around, admiring my fine leather coat, acknowledging my entrance. Girls would want to dance with me and guys would treat me like one of the in-crowd at last.

It took me almost two hours to make it to the north side, by train and bus. I was so hyped up I could have probably run the entire way. As I arrived at the final stop and headed toward the address of the party, a thought ran across my mind: not many young black guys could be found in this neighborhood at this time of night, so I must be either the most courageous or stupidest kid east of the Mississippi River. You just didn't trespass onto another group's part of town after certain hours.

I finally got to the house, walked up the front steps, and found the door ajar. I walked in not to thunderous applause but to blank stares. I quickly realized I was one of the few black kids at the party (the others were mostly from the football team). I felt like turning around and getting the hell out. But before I could, I felt a hand on my shoulder. It was my friend, the host. "Hey, James, I'm glad you came," he said with a smile. At that moment I would have followed him anywhere—but he soon disappeared into the crowd. Trying my best to look casual, I decided to park myself in front of a keg of beer, where I stood for quite some time. People walked past me as if I wasn't even there. Kids I knew from class ignored me. I felt completely out of place. The night had morphed into the opposite of how I'd imagined it would go.

I drank a lot of beer but didn't like it. I didn't like any-thing that was happening at the party. The music was unbearably loud. The rooms were so crowded I could hardly move and I was carelessly bumped and jostled. It was like I was a piece of furniture out of place. People were yelling, and the football players were rowdy. I watched a girl stumble past in a drunken stupor. I remember telling myself that if this was how the popular kids lived, I was glad I wasn't one of them. I kept thinking that my mother was right in telling me not to go. I stood there alone, waiting for the party to end, but instead it went on and on. Finally, when I couldn't stand another minute, I made my way to the door—stealthily, being careful not to attract attention—and slipped out into the cold, telling myself that I would feel better once I got to bed.

I took the bus to the elevated train and fell asleep, somehow awakening exactly at my stop. The platform was empty except for a small group of guys standing at the top of the stairs. They were black like me, but that was no comfort. As I approached, one of them said, "Damn, that's a cool coat." I knew it was a threat, not a compliment. Another asked if I had any money so they could ride "the el." I told them I didn't. "Then we'll take your coat."

"No way," I said. I would never give up that token of love my father had given me. I thought I could bluff my way through, but they wouldn't take no for an answer. I don't clearly recall what happened next, but it quickly got violent and I felt a knife going into my left side. A few hours later I was found unconscious in the snow below the stairs, bleeding and without my coat.

I was taken to Cook County Hospital and pronounced dead on arrival. They put my body on a gurney next to a wall in a corridor. Slipping into and out of consciousness, I don't know how long I lay there before a nurse happened to notice my arm hanging down with blood dripping from it. She felt for a pulse and discovered I was still alive! I was rushed to surgery, and they sewed up the left side of my body. I remember waking up and seeing my mother and thinking: Oh no! Now she knows I snuck out of the house. But she never spoke a word of her anger and disappointment. She was totally forgiving and prayed for me every night.

They put me in the Critical Care ward and determined I was paralyzed from the neck down. I also had frostbite so severe that they told my mother my foot would have to be amputated. I cried and begged her to stop them. She talked with the doctors and they decided against it. I was greatly relieved, but still paralyzed with no guarantees I would ever recover. Days later, I was transferred to another hospital. This new hospital seemed much better.

My mother was a constant presence at my bedside from start to finish, though I don't know how she managed it while working every day and taking care of her other children. She wouldn't leave me alone in a strange place knowing what I was going through; she tried to make me as comfortable as possible. She was a real angel. I'll always regret being such a source of pain and grief for her.

Chapter Two

Dark Rooms and Heavy Air

The doctors came in every day to poke my feet and toes with needles and ask if I felt anything. I was terrified because I wasn't feeling any pain. This went on for several weeks. The worst part was watching the nurse who changed the bandages on the left side of my body. She was the most-cold hearted person I had ever seen, smiling as she literally ripped the bandages away from my wounds. I couldn't feel pain, but the way she yanked them felt sadistic, as if she got some weird pleasure from the process.

Finally, one day, as the doctor began his pin-sticking, I felt something sharp. "Doc," I said, shocked and hopeful, "I think I felt something." He stuck me again, and I triumphantly cried "Ouch!" Within minutes, it seemed like every doctor in the hospital was crowded into my small room. There was so much conversation going on in so many different languages that I couldn't understand a word. Later, I found out that it was a teaching hospital with medical students from all over the world.

In the days and weeks to come, feeling slowly advanced through my entire body. It was amazing and in some mysterious way, I think the cold-hearted nurse's behavior may have helped. Even though I couldn't feel what she was doing, I had imagined the pain of it, and maybe that experience had triggered something. Unfortunately, even after the feeling returned to my body, the same nurse changed the bandages with the same sadistic gusto. The knife wound had not yet healed, and it felt as if the skin was being ripped from my bones. I wouldn't have been surprised if she had made bets with the hospital staff that she could make me scream. If so, she won, for scream I did.

After many months, I was finally allowed to leave the hospital, though I still couldn't fully walk, and I would require a lengthy process of rehabilitation. My mother didn't think it was safe for me to return to the neighborhood where we lived, so she sent me to stay with my father on the far south side.

I had never lived with my father and didn't know what to expect. He was good-looking, confident, and knew how to dress, always attracting positive attention wherever he went. He was living the bachelor's life with lots of girlfriends. Needless to say, having a teenage son in the apartment cramped his style. He endured it because he had been an absent father and must have seen this as a second chance. I could see he wanted to be helpful and do things right, but parenting was new to him. I felt out of place. His environment was not conducive to the sensitive recovery of a wounded teenager.

And yet in some primitive way, it may have been motivational. I wasn't used to hearing the sounds of sexual activity every night, the squeaking bed and women shouting in ecstasy. The smell of raw, uninhibited lovemaking was new to me, musty with a tinge of sweetness. Dark rooms and heavy air. A part of me was mesmerized. I wanted to learn how to pleasure women the way my father did. But how could I ever be like him? How could I even get a date? I couldn't move without the use of a wheelchair and, later, crutches. I could dream, though, and my dreams were vivid. I convinced myself that all I needed was experience and believed that I would find my own way.

One day a sympathetic Lane friend, Theresa, came to my father's house to visit me. She was almost seventeen and already quite womanly. My father and his friends pointed her toward my room. When she came into my room and closed the door behind her, I could imagine them thinking "Wow, little fat boy is pretty lucky." But all Theresa did was sit on my bed and ask what happened. I told her the whole story, and then summed it up by saying I should have listened to my mother.

It didn't take long before I yearned to return to my mother's house. She had a natural ability to make a person feel special and I wanted to be with her. She must have heard my cries and told my father to bring me back. I loved my father and wanted to spend as much time with him as I could but there weren't many opportunities. He was too busy working during the day, hanging with his friends, and making love at night. I knew even then that he meant well, but he was too used to the way things were before I showed up. And so, after a few months with my father and finally mastering walking again, I returned home.

There was no Wizard of Oz moment of clicking my heels and returning to a peaceful little farm. Back on the southwest side of Chicago I found the same rundown streets and a crowded apartment in a crowded neighborhood; the exploding sounds of sirens and the cries of the suffering. I had become so used to that life that I hadn't realized how much suffering there was—for my family, neighbors, and community. It took the comfort of distance for a while for that stinging truth to slap me awake!

I had missed the entire last half of the school year and now summer was ending. I was walking without crutches, but my gait was still awkward. One bright spot was my appearance: as a result of being bedridden and the lengthy recovery process, I had lost weight. Not a lot, but enough to notice and it felt good. The new school year was approaching quickly, and all the kids were buying their fall attire. In a normal year, I'd be working to buy my own clothes, but now, I wasn't in good enough shape. In the past I would buy the coolest outfits to compensate for self-consciousness about my weight, but now I couldn't afford my own taste and agonized over what to wear. My worries about style, however, were soon replaced by a bigger problem.

The school had contacted my mother and explained that because I had missed so much of the last year, I would need to repeat my junior year in order to get credit towards graduation. I thought this was unfair. I didn't want to lose an entire year. I wanted to graduate with my class. My mother explained that there was nothing we could do, but if I was willing to repeat the year I would still be able to graduate from Lane. Unfortunately, my ego and self-esteem were too fragile for that. To lose a year and watch my classmates go on to become upperclassmen wasn't acceptable and I pleaded to be spared that humiliation. My mother, already stressed by trying to raise her children, work, and honor her marriage to my latest stepfather, finally gave in. I could attend the neighborhood school without having to repeat any classes. I would graduate on time and my ego would remain intact.

She enlisted the aid of a woman who lived upstairs to make me a new double-knit suit to wear on my first day. I'd been talking about clothing so much that my mother hoped this would relieve some of my anxiety of attending a new high school. And it helped until I arrived. Then the reality of my new environment took over.

A dark-skinned black man in a red double-knit suit on a hot day in inner city Chicago is not a good look. The teasing began almost immediately and my reaction, prompted by the rage of my low self-esteem, was to challenge everyone to a fight. One guy obliged me almost as soon as the last word left my mouth. A group of students quickly formed to watch the new kid fight. In a school like this, the kids didn't judge you on your smarts; they judged you on how well you could fight. The noise of the crowd got louder and more intense. The majority seemed to be pulling for the other kid to beat the hell out of me, so I kept him at a distance by taking wide, heavy swings. The circle of people around us got larger and tighter, drawing the attention of a teacher and a security guard who came over and stopped us. So, my first day at the new school turned out to be a fashion disaster followed by a bad conduct violation.

The following days weren't much better. The school building was dilapidated. The walls were full of graffiti—not smart or artful graffiti—just dirty. Classrooms were chaotic with little opportunity for any real learning. The reading materials were outdated and torn. One class used a book I had read in my freshman year two years earlier at the better school on the other side of town. Every day felt like a battle for survival as teachers tried to survive the day without incident while the kids did whatever they felt like. Some came just to hang out, shoot dice behind the school, smoke weed, or make out with their girlfriends on the stairs. It was very depressing. How could a school system allow this to happen? Each day I became more and more disenchanted with pursuing an education. I was just going through the motions and it all felt like a tremendous waste of time.

A friend of mine—one of my few—suggested joining the military, which got me thinking about starting a new life in the Marine Corps. My older brother had enlisted in the marines a year before and he seemed to be doing well. The more I thought about it, the better I felt; I needed a way to escape where I was and the service seemed like the perfect opportunity.

We went to the recruiter's office together and filled out the papers, signing up on the buddy system, which ensured that we would be sent to the same base for Basic Training. We were fully prepared to leave for the military that day! The recruiter looked over the documents and told my friend that everything was in order. Then he looked at me and said there was a problem: I had put the wrong age on the form. You had to be eighteen to enlist and I had written seventeen. He handed me the form and the pen. I wasn't sure what to do. I didn't feel comfortable lying.

My friend pulled me outside and told me to quit acting like an idiot. "It's simple," he said. "Change the 7 to an 8. It's the only way we'll get into the Corps together." We walked back into the recruiter's office and sat down. "Are you ready to write your age on this form?" the recruiter asked, sliding the pen toward me again. I asked if there was some other way to sign up. "Only one," he said. "You would need your mother to sign the papers." I knew that was a near impossibility, but I just couldn't lie. I told my friend that I needed to talk to my mother. He shrugged and said,

"Whatever!" and the recruiter handed me the forms for my mother to sign.

I arrived at home with the forms in my hand and went directly to the kitchen where my mother and her sister were having a serious conversation. That ended when I told them I wanted to join the Marine Corps. They looked at each other and burst out laughing. When their eruption of laughter died down, their words seemed more matter of fact. They pointed out that I'd only been out of the hospital a few months and that I should wait to be fully healed before making such a huge decision. My mother's sister reminded me that six months ago I couldn't even walk. Their faces changed when I insisted that there was nothing for me in that high school, that it was a dead end. I wanted more out of life than wasting time in a school that wasn't teaching me anything. My passion expressed itself as free-flowing tears. My mother realized it wasn't a good time to make such a decision in the midst of high emotions and tabled the discussion until the next morning.

I woke up early to find her sitting at the kitchen table in the same position she was in when I went to bed. She was drinking a cup of coffee, and as I sat down, it seemed that my mother had aged overnight. I begged her not to worry but insisted that I had to go. She said she never wanted to sit by my bedside in a hospital ever again. I promised that I would take care of myself and begged her to sign the papers. She took a long sip of coffee and let out a deep sigh. It's never an easy moment when someone who loves you deeply must make a decision that their heart doesn't agree with. Painfully, reluctantly, my mother scribbled her signature on the forms releasing me into the service. I took them back to the recruiter that day and enlisted in the Marine Corps. My buddy was already gone.

For the next couple of months while waiting for Boot Camp, I worked out every day, running and doing push-ups, desperately trying to prepare for the tough, legendary pressure—mental and physical—the Corps puts their recruits through. I was still overweight and still recovering from my injuries, but I had to make it through Boot Camp because there was nothing else left for me. Failure was not an option. Like a gambler, I was "all in."

This is the attitude I showed up with, ready for whatever it would take to make it through. And sure enough, the drill instructors were on me like bees on honey. They called me every kind of name in the book. "City Slicker" (since I was from Chicago) was one of the better ones; the worst was "Chocolate Pillsbury Dough Boy," bestowed on me by a drill instructor of German heritage (I didn't say "Nazi" but I sure thought it sometimes). It was so degrading that the other drill instructors wouldn't use it. I felt terrible every time I heard it but knew enough to bite my tongue and do as I was told. And I was told to do a lot—so much that it often felt like they were picking on me. It turned out they were—but for good reason. I didn't realize it at the time, but the drill instructors instinctively knew that I desperately wanted to complete Boot Camp, so they gave me extra attention and did everything they could to pound me into shape—all the more difficult because of my weight. When, for example, a recruit who broke a rule or didn't follow orders was punished with extra exercises, I was included for no reason. The strategy worked: by the end of the three-month camp I'd lost an astonishing fifty pounds, dropping to 135 from 185, which looked mighty good on my five-and-a-half-foot frame. At the graduation ceremony, while standing at attention in our dress blues on the parade deck, the instructor of German descent called me out in front of the entire platoon: "Won't your mother be proud of you!" I felt touched and proud (and maybe a little embarrassed about how mentally uncharitable I'd been to him).

My first duty station was a military base in Okinawa, Japan, thousands of miles and an ocean away from the housing projects of Chicago. The island of Okinawa was sarcastically known as "the Rock" by U.S. servicemen. I had the good fortune of landing at one of the better bases, but it was still a lonely place. My mates and I developed a camaraderie and a natural closeness, which grew out of being so far from home together, but they were neither my real family nor the kind of guys I'd grown up with. Still, we did everything we could to make it bearable, each of us finding our own way to cope with life "on the Rock." Some found solace in the military base chapel, which they would earnestly attend on Sunday mornings and some nights after work. They would read the Bible and take every opportunity to share what they'd learned with anyone willing to listen. I remember asking one of them, "Why does God send

His people through so much heartache and pain in life?" His answer made me take notice. "God must strengthen you, and since you have free will, you must go through it and know that you can handle anything. God won't put more on you than you can bear." I have given considerable thought to those words throughout my life since and know the truth of them now, but that was achieved only after considerably more heartache and pain.

Other guys escaped through alcohol. They took great joy shopping at the Post Exchange (the base store) for their allotted bottles. The Marine brass didn't seem to care, and it was almost expected that the booze would start flowing Friday night and continue through Sunday. However, you had better be sober and hopefully, clean and bathed by Monday morning. I didn't drink but did have my own allotment of alcohol, so I'd make deals, buying and distributing my alcohol for extra cash. The drinkers appreciated my help and thought I was a good guy. It paid to be sober, a useful lesson.

Then there were the bullies. They couldn't deal with their loneliness or sadness; the only emotion they could express was anger. They preferred to fight the world because they couldn't face themselves. The bullies would find any reason to vent: attacking the guys who talked about the Bible; the guys who boozed it up; or just guys who were smaller than them, whom they knew they could push around.

I had been on the rock for almost three months when an incident occurred that had me throwing up for days. There was a Christian Marine, a skinny white guy, always talking up the Bible. He was so persistent that he had irritated and alienated almost everyone in the unit. People would walk the other way when they saw him coming. One day, in formation, he made a terrible mistake. The platoon lieutenant reprimanded him for talking. The skinny Christian said he was only speaking God's words. The lieutenant told him to shut up. The Christian kid responded that the lieutenant was going to Hell. That night inside the barracks, the Christian was slapped hard in the face by one of the toughest sergeants on the rock. I know that the kid didn't want to fight this monster, but a slap is worse than someone bad-mouthing your mother, and so he had no other choice except to swing back.

It wasn't a fight, it was a slaughter, the most frightening I'd ever seen. I had a ringside seat to the animalistic manner in which human beings can treat one another. No one tried to stop it. No one said a word—including, I'm ashamed to say, me. Even as the sergeant slammed the skinny kid to the floor and sat on top of him, pounding his face, no one intervened, even as the blood was flowing.

I remember walking away before the beating was over, but the images were burned into my memory. In my bunk that night, I wondered if the kid would live or die. I got ill just imagining how much pain he must have been in. No one reported the incident. It stayed hushed up inside the unit. One compassionate Marine slowly nursed the kid back to health. He stayed in the barracks, out of sight, until enough time had passed that his physical wounds healed. No one ever questioned why he wasn't present at formations or for other duties, though everyone knew what had happened. The official story was that he had staggered into the barracks, drunk, and slipped on some soapy water, busting his head. That was life on the rock.

It was a great day when I got my orders to return to the United States. I felt like a kid at Christmas about to open his gifts. I was headed for California and kept imagining all the good times I would have there. I'd heard about California: the girls, the ocean, the movie stars, the City of Angels. It didn't occur to me that not every woman actually looked like a model and that people would not treat you like a celebrity unless you were one. I just knew I was getting out of Hell, so I must be headed for Paradise.

My older brother, Ronald, and his wife were stationed at the Marine Corps base at Camp Pendleton in California. He had planned early on to make a career in the military. In high school, he joined the Reserve Officers' Training Corps (ROTC) and wore that uniform with pride. He was tough and confident and wasn't swayed by what was popular, caring little about what other people considered cool or not. He had a one-track mind and a plan, and no one was going to throw him off his game. I did not possess such clarity and self-confidence; I was still trying to please others and be liked. Oh, how I wish now I had been more like my brother then.

Chapter Three

A Day I Will Never Forget and Will Always Regret

California! I arrived in San Diego without fanfare. There was no cheering crowd waiting for my plane to land, no girlfriend to welcome me with a kiss. The Marines didn't even pick me up. I found my way to base and checked in with my Commanding Officer. I was shown where to sleep and eat. I was told what time to arrive for formation and what time would be my own. The sleeping quarters were cramped; instead of a lengthy barracks with bunks stacked on both sides like in Okinawa, I was shown to a small room that I would share with two other young Marines—though not as young as me. It seemed that I was always the youngest in the room, not surprising since I joined the Corps at seventeen and was still barely twenty.

My roommates were rowdy. They would bring beer into the room after hours and drink and curse all night. Of course, this was against the rules, but they didn't care. Marines had a certain swagger that was admired and feared by other military people. I admit I had some of it myself. We accepted without question that we were the toughest dudes on the planet. We could kick ass from one country to the next. That's how we were trained to think, an indoctrination that began in Boot Camp and never let up. Other branches of the military also seemed to believe that Marines were the hardcore craziest, a belief and expectation that we did our best to confirm. Marines didn't take any shit. We believed we were indestructible. One thing about Marines always remained true: even if they were beating the hell out of you, you could call on another Marine and he would help you. That was the meaning of "Semper Fidelis." We were always faithful to the Corps and each other—Semper Fi.

My brother tried to be helpful and show me around, but he was often busy attending his pregnant wife. She had a brother of her own nearby, also a Marine and also from Chicago. He was a popular guy with a charismatic coolness that people wanted to be around. He and his girlfriend threw huge parties at their off-base apartment. They had lots of friends and knew how to show them a good time. I felt grateful that he often invited me (my brother had better things to do): The music was loud, there was plenty to drink, and it all kept me from feeling lonely. Alcohol, however, wasn't the only intoxicant available. I soon found out that my brother's brother-in-law (I'll call him Ricky) was involved in a lot more than wild parties.

Since I had my own car (a used Pontiac I had bought for my off-duty hours) Ricky would ask me to get ice, beer, or chips whenever they started running out. I was willing to be the gofer because I wanted to feel part of the scene, even though I was uncomfortable with my role and often with the scene itself. Ricky and his crowd were the only friends I had, even though in truth I barely knew them.

March 15, 1983 is the day I will never forget and always regret. I had just completed my daily Marine Corps assignment (Non-com in charge of communications equipment) and was taking what I thought would be a long, hot shower when I heard a loud knock at the door. I tried to ignore it but it became louder and more insistent. "Give me a minute!" I yelled, grabbing a towel. Dripping with water and moving toward the door, I noticed an unsettling feeling in my stomach. When I opened the door, I was surprised to see Ricky standing there, out of uniform and perspiring, looking dead serious. I let him in and listened as he told me an incredible story. Ricky confessed to owing a man named Damiano a lot of money for drugs he was supposed to have been selling but instead had used himself. He told me he'd given him a partial payment but Damiano threatened to kill him if he didn't come up with the rest of the money. He wanted to go to Damiano's apartment, scare him, and recover some personal items he had given as collateral for the drugs. "We can't let this guy get away with threatening a Marine!" he said. He assured me that he wanted to quit using and selling and that this would be his last deal.

Unfortunately, he didn't have a way to get there and needed me to drive him. Well, Ricky was a Marine and so was I. So I pulled on a pair of sweats and a T-shirt and followed him to the parking lot. Three of Ricky's friends were already standing by my car, none of whom I knew. He said they were coming with us.

Without questioning anything, I dutifully followed Ricky's directions to Damiano's apartment. There was a Marine-mission-like feeling to the trip and conversation was sparse. At one point, Ricky suddenly told me to turn left as I was turning right, so I crossed two lanes of traffic to make the turn. Right away I saw the flashing lights of a police car in the rearview mirror. One of the guys in the back seat panicked. "The police is pulling us over!" Ricky told everybody to stay calm. I complied. The officer approached my side of the car and asked for my driver's license and registration. I complied. He walked back to his squad car. It obviously didn't look good: five black guys in a car that had just swerved through traffic would normally raise plenty of red flags. But in a Marine Corps town, blacks driving in groups was not uncommon. In fact, it seemed as if the town appreciated us being there and spending our meager military checks. "Nobody act nervous," I remember Ricky saying. I complied. After several excruciating minutes, the officer walked back and handed me a ticket for making an illegal lane change. "Please drive safely," he said, then turned and walked back to his squad car. Had he searched the vehicle, he would have found Ricky's shotgun, which I never knew was there. That would have changed everything.

Shaken but undeterred, we continued toward Damiano's apartment. As we rolled into the parking lot, the same unsettling feeling I'd felt earlier returned to my stomach. I parked the car, waiting for instructions from Ricky. He lifted a brown leather bag from between his legs and we all got out. He walked to the front of the car and pointed at the biggest of the three other guys. "You'll knock on the door, and when Damiano opens it, James goes in and tells everyone to get on the floor." He then pulled a sawed-off shotgun out of the bag, loaded both barrels, and handed it to me. He told the big guy to signal him outside the door when I had everyone on the floor.

Me? I was numb with fear. But I was a Marine. I knew weapons but only on a target range. And this was only a civilian "persuader." Perhaps it would all work out okay.

I followed the big guy onto the porch. I could hear his heart pounding against his massive chest. I held the shotgun down by my side. My grip was tight, my finger on the trigger. I did not know that the "persuader" had a hair trigger. He knocked on the door. It opened. The Big Guy moved to the side and I quickly walked in. In my peripheral vision I saw a guy getting up from the kitchen table. Turning in his direction, I lifted my arm to show him I had a gun—and it went off! The BOOM was shockingly loud. The big guy behind me screamed while the man getting up from the table fell backwards onto the floor. Seconds seemed like hours. I was stunned. What had just happened?

I'd awakened that morning like any other morning, had a day like every other day, and now my world was upside down. It made no sense, but I couldn't undo what I had just done. One life was lost, and another forever changed in that single moment of violence. I heard my car starting and peeling off, which startled me back to reality. Stumbling back through the door, I saw it speeding through the complex and I cut across a yard to intercept it. Ricky was driving so I jumped in on the passenger side. I kept repeating, "It wasn't supposed to happen like that. It wasn't supposed to happen like that." Inside the car was chaos, everyone talking at once. The big guy was in the back seat, crying. The others wanted to get out of the car and away from me— the guy who had just killed someone. It was still totally unreal to me to think that I could have done this, the last thing in the world I ever thought would happen. But it had.

We dropped off one guy who wanted out at the first safe opportunity. We let out another guy at his girlfriend's off-base apartment; he took the shotgun to hide. The only people left were Ricky, the big guy, and me. As we approached the entrance to the Marine Corps base, I felt my stomach churning. The security guard waved us in and another directed us to pull over. Within minutes the car was surrounded by San Diego County sheriffs with guns drawn, shouting commands. I am still amazed that people think you can understand what they are saying while they're pointing a gun at you.

They got us out of the car, one at a time, and handcuffed us. They were in no rush. They took each of us by a different squad car to the police station and locked us in different interview rooms. We were grilled by detectives until the early morning hours. When they got tired, then we spoke to more detectives. The Marine Corps maxim to "Only give your name, rank, and serial number to your captors" had been drilled deep inside my psyche where I stored it right next to the street code I'd learned in Chicago: to never tell authority figures what you saw or heard. And so I remained quiet and stoic throughout the entire process; numb actually, observing, in a state of unreality. I found out later this wasn't the case for the big guy who was singing like a hungry parrot looking at a cracker.

We were taken to the county jail and photographed, finger-printed, and relieved of all personal property. They put us in sections of the jail called "housing units" but they were nothing like houses. They were noisy and filthy. Ricky was placed in the same unit as me; the big guy went to a different one.

In the days, weeks, and months that followed, I received a graduate degree in the workings of the California criminal justice system. I couldn't afford an attorney, so I was given one by the Public Defender's office, which was funded by the State of California—the same entity that was also paying for my prosecution. The money available for my defense was meager compared to the budget for the prosecution, and my legal representative hardly resembled a dream-team like Johnny Cochran and Robert Kardashian working the angles for O.J. Simpson.

I had a self-serving attorney who (it turned out) was more interested in how much more money he could make from a lengthy trial than justice or fair representation. He didn't care, for example, that the shooting was the unintended result of a hair trigger. When that gun went off and that unfortunate human being hit the floor, I was stunned. I had no idea that the weapon would discharge so easily, and it certainly had never been my intention to do anything but support a brother Marine. True, I shouldn't have been pointing a gun at anyone, but my intention was only to "persuade." That I had killed a man was devastating, but none of this mattered to the man charged with defending me. His only "concern," as he explained one day, was to save my life since I could face the death penalty. None of this mattered to me since I was dead inside already.

During the long wait in the San Diego County Jail, I was so guilt ridden for taking a man's life that I performed only the most basic of human functions on auto-pilot. I was locked up mentally as well as physically. I was numb.

I can remember my mother flying out to visit me while I was in the San Diego County jail. It was depressing and heart wrenching; imagine disappointment after disappointment magnified a thousand times. My father flew out to San Diego a couple of times and seemed more reticent.

My brother visited me and was always very angry about the entire situation.

I spent nearly a year in jail awaiting trial—an unusual length of time then, but now, almost commonplace. By the time my trial actually started, the District Attorney had decided not to pursue the death penalty but did seek a first-degree murder conviction. Knowing I would live, shocked me back into a kind of normalcy, but that feeling didn't last long. If convicted of first-degree murder, my future would still be bleak. I'd be facing life in prison, or at best, 25 years before any chance of being released.

The trial consisted of testimony from Damiano (under the protection of immunity) and statements from expert witnesses including psychologists testifying to my mental state. A weapons expert witness confirmed that the gun had a very light trigger pull and police authorities had their say. My commanding officer and other members from my unit stood up in my defense because I had a nearly perfect record as a Marine. I had been meritoriously promoted and received the Humanitarian Service Award when I was deployed overseas. I knew I was guilty of taking a life, but I was hoping that the circumstances of my crime would somehow afford me some leniency—though I had no idea of what kind. I was never informed, for example, that California law had two other options besides first-degree murder for someone accused of taking a life: second-degree murder and manslaughter. The penalty for second-degree murder was the possibility of parole after 15 years. The maximum penalty for manslaughter at the time of my crime was six years (since increased to 11), but apparently these were insignificant details to my attorney.

The trial lasted several months. In the end, the jury couldn't agree on a first-degree murder conviction. It turned out that the holdouts were the only three women on the jury. Apparently, they had to endure scorn and verbal abuse from the nine men who were ready to flush my life away. When the jury first informed the judge that they couldn't reach a verdict, he sent them back to the jury room with more instructions. They returned sometime later without a decision and one of the women complained about the treatment they were receiving from the men. The judge read more instructions and sent them back again to continue their deliberations. On the sixth day, the jury went back to the judge and said they were hopelessly dead-locked. One of the women declared she could no longer stand the abuse she was getting in the jury room from the men. I know this because it was all declared in open court. The judge finally ruled a mistrial. Those women didn't know me prior to this trial but something must have touched their hearts and given them the strength to resist the pressure to convict. I still thank God for their courage to stand their ground and give me a second chance at life.

My father had come from Chicago to attend the trial. He had some insight into the criminal justice process and told me there wouldn't be a second trial because the District Attorney would offer me a plea bargain instead. And that's what happened; the DA invited me to plead guilty to voluntary manslaughter. Any reasonable attorney would have advised any client facing first-degree murder charges, to take the deal. (At the time, a conviction of manslaughter meant six years in prison, a fact no one, certainly not my attorney, explained to me.) My attorney advised me not to take the plea bargain. He emphasized that we had "proven" our case in the first trial and that it would be even easier to do it again. My father had gone back to Chicago and I was still dazed, recovering from what I'd done and deeply shaken by my ordeal in jail. I was in no condition to make a crucial decision that would have life-changing consequences. And so, following my attorney's advice, I declined the DA's offer. As the guards were taking me from the conference room, I overheard my attorney tell the DA that he'd be able to buy another car after the second trial ended.

I found out later that Ricky had taken a plea deal, which meant about three years in prison. The big guy who testified for the prosecution was also given a deal and spent one year in the county jail; the guy who hid the gun had the charges against him dropped because of a lack of evidence; and the fifth guy never faced charges.

The District Attorney re-filed the charges against me and a second trial was scheduled. This time he made sure there weren't three women on the jury.

The second trial felt like a repeat of the first, including most of the same witnesses and lasted the same amount of time. I had felt overwhelmed and depressed during the first trial, but paid a lot more attention during the second, where the primary issue now was whether or not I had intended to commit a robbery in the intentional or unintentional commission of a homicide. I started to feel hopeful, though the DA was still seeking a first-degree murder conviction. Finally, the case was placed in the hands of the mostly male jury with only one woman. After eight days of deliberations, the jury asked if they could find me guilty of a lesser charge. The trial court judge reiterated the jury instructions, and before he sent the jury members back, the DA urged them to find me guilty of something, at least second-degree murder. And that's what they did, returning almost immediately with that exact conviction. The mandatory sentence was imposed: 15 years to life. Next stop: Soledad Prison.

Chapter Four

Waking to the Nightmare

My introduction to the reality of prison life began as soon as I arrived at Soledad in 1985. My cellmate was a big, slow-thinking, older guy from Alabama called Fat Joe who had a thing for pruno—prison wine. He had convinced himself that he was a wine connoisseur, and each week he would collect the fruit left over from Sunday breakfast, usually oranges or grapefruits. He would squeeze the juice out and mix it with sugar and yeast, wrap the concoction in blankets, stick it under his bed to ferment, and then strain it on Friday and start drinking. By Saturday night the pruno would be gone, and Fat Joe would be blotto.

At first, I just considered the guy an oddball—the pruno was more like solvent than wine—but it didn't take long before I was helping him collect the ingredients and guzzling that poison down, seeking some escape from the despair and loneliness of my situation. Two years earlier I had been doing well, in the Marine Corps, imagining a future, and now I was gripped in the inescapable hell of concrete walls—a prison packed tightly with wailing, seething souls. Sounds of terror and torment filled the days and nights. I was twenty-two years old and my sanity was shaken to its core. The pruno offered the illusion of escape, but as the weeks and months went by, it became increasingly clear (to others, anyway) that I was slowly killing myself.

An inmate named Russell pulled me over one day and asked if I had looked in a mirror lately. Without waiting for an answer, he took me to the barber's room and stood me in front of one. I couldn't believe it was me; I had become unrecognizable. My beard had grown wildly, my hair was unkempt, and my skin looked pale and dry. I had aged twenty years. Russell said I had to get out of that cell or I would surely die there. The next day I told Fat Joe that I was moving to another cell. He took it personally and became very upset. He put on his workout gloves, tied on his boots, then stood up and challenged me to a fight. I weighed 150 pounds soaking wet and this guy was at least 250. I knew I wouldn't stand a chance in that cramped space so I decided to outthink him. I kept my emotions and tongue in-check and calmly told him that I didn't realize he wanted me to be his cellmate so badly. I told him I'd stay that night and that I appreciated him showing how much he cared about me. He took off his gloves and asked if I wanted some pruno.

The next morning, Russell paid the housing clerk two packs of cigarettes to move me into his cell. The usual move-out procedure is for an inmate to fill out a move request form, give it to the sergeant to sign, and then wait about two weeks for a decision. Inmates who have resources can shorten the process, and while Russell didn't have money, he knew other ways to get things done. Although his outer appearance was strong—he had a chiseled physique and masculine features—Russell was quite humble. His eyes told the story of a man who had lived a tough life and learned hard lessons. Above all, he had tremendous compassion for young African Americans and a revolutionary character in the spirit of Malcolm X, Angela Davis, and Che Guevara. People knew that when Russell said he would do something, it would get done. He was a respected and no-nonsense guy.

When Fat Joe found out I had moved into the cell with Russell, he never spoke to me again. Russell was all about reality. He kept his body in fighting shape and stayed mentally ready for the eventuality of prison drama. He never smoked and never drank pruno. Russell inspired me to get on the right track and I started doing push-ups and taking care of my body. I learned a lot from him in the short time we shared a cell. There's nothing like being stuck in a small space with someone every day to discover things about yourself you might have forgotten, overlooked, or didn't want to know. There is nowhere to run or hide. Russell saw the truth of who I was and what I was going through, not the public face I put on for the other inmates. He heard me crying as I slept. He saw a young man suffocating in guilt and self-pity—someone who couldn't forgive himself for taking the life of another human being in such a senseless way and ruining his own life at the same time.

I wanted the prison world to see a tough Marine but in fact I was paralyzed by remorse and rage. Russell responded like the wise and compassionate mentor he was. He taught me about the Moors of 700 A.D. and how they brought inclusiveness, religious tolerance, and enlightenment to the people of Spain and later Southern Italy. He also taught me about Sun Tzu, the Chinese warrior-philosopher of 2000 years ago, emphasizing his famous quote, "To overcome the other's armies without fighting is the best of all skills." Russell worked on my self- esteem. He constantly applauded my intelligence and eagerness to learn, and encouraged me to work out, getting my body back in shape.

Three months later he was paroled to Fresno to reunite with his wife and kids, and I missed him, but I had learned more in those three months with Russell than I had ever learned from any teacher previously. After Russell left, I felt more self-assured and physically powerful. And while it's true that a little knowledge can get you out of trouble, it can also get you into trouble. My newfound confidence led me to hanging out with some men who didn't have Russell's steadiness or moral compass.

One day five of us were sitting on the ground playing poker in the rec area—a closely watched, open-air space commonly known as "the yard." I was the youngest and least experienced but wasn't getting hustled because I was tight with Red, the guy running the game. One day, one of the players, a slender Cuban I'd never met, accused Red of cheating. He spoke fast and reached anger easily. His English wasn't great, but he was fluent in profanity. I said something like, "Hey, we're just trying to have a friendly game here," and he turned on me, accusing me of working with Red. He jumped up, kicked Red in the head and, before I could stand, kicked me in the face and ran off. We were all too dazed and startled to mount any kind of a fight. If we tried to chase him, we risked getting shot by the guards in the gun towers. I was bleeding pretty badly from a broken nose and needed attention. When a guard stopped me and asked about my injury, I said, "It happened on the basketball court." He sent me to the infirmary where medical employees stopped the bleeding and sent me back to my cell. The Sergeant on duty ordered that I be confined to my cell for twenty-four hours until he could investigate the matter further.

That night, members from two different African-American gangs came to the bars of my cell. Since the inmate who kicked me was from Cuba, the incident was looked upon as an "Other" attacking a "Black." This meant I would have to retaliate not just for my own respect but for my race. They slipped me a flat metal bar that was filed down to a knife blade: my weapon. The gang members made it very clear that if I got cold feet and didn't use it, they would use it on me. I had to choose: attack or be attacked. It meant risking my life either way. Another lesson in how cheap human life was behind these walls. Here I was, facing a potentially fatal decision, just by being in the wrong place at the wrong time.

I paced all night playing out different scenarios in my head, trying to imagine a way to get through the situation with the least heartache and pain. I was still considering my options when the guard unlocked my cell for morning breakfast. My mind raced, filled with more questions than answers. Why are the guards violating the Sergeant's orders and letting me out of my cell? Should I just stay inside? What if I stab the Cuban and he dies? What will the black gangs do to me if I don't? I finally decided to just scratch the Cuban guy with the knife to show effort, and hope that would satisfy the gangs. I didn't consider that the guy wouldn't just stand there while I attacked.

I finally left the cell and walked slowly against the wall waiting for the Cuban inmate to appear. I saw him enter the corridor ahead of me and start walking toward the dining hall. In my mind, I had pictured the way the stabbing would go, but of course things never happen the way you imagine them. When I finally got close enough I lunged at him. He turned instinctively but he was too late, and my knife found the side of his body. He let out a scream, but I think more from shock and surprise than pain because I knew I hadn't struck deep. He flailed his hands at me and I hit him again with the makeshift knife. Other inmates kept walking by as if nothing was happening. The guards, however, began running toward us. I threw the knife across the floor. The guards grabbed us, cuffed us, and took us to separate examination rooms in the infirmary. When questioned about what happened, we both remained silent. That was the usual protocol. Even though he had just been attacked, the Cuban still followed the unwritten prisoner's code of silence—just as I had the day before.

Neither of us needed stitches, though I was bleeding worse than he was because the makeshift handle of my weapon had sliced into the palm of my hand. I found it ironic that blood oozed out of me when I was attacked and then again when I was the attacker.

The medical report confirmed the superficiality of the Cuban's wounds, but the guards skewed their reports to make the incident sound like the most vicious in Soledad's history. Our blood-stained clothing was sequestered in the evidence locker and all movement in and around the prison was halted by order of the Warden. He wanted to know whether the incident was the prelude to a race riot. Such "incident investigations" are usually conducted in the same way in every prison. While the prison is on lockdown, guards bring out inmates one cell at a time. The guards will conduct up to fifty interviews a day, and lockdowns can last many weeks.

During these times, the guards receive hazardous duty and overtime pay, and the prison's budget increases in anticipation of future "incidents." Prison administrators are always on the lookout for opportunities to keep the money flowing.

And so, they interviewed a number of inmates to determine the cause and likely impacts of my attack and confirmed virtually every detail of what happened, from start to finish. The "code of silence" is obviously violated in such instances, because it is difficult to nail down which inmates informed about what took place and who, why, and where it happened. It was common knowledge that certain inmates "worked" with the guards. This keeps the administration up-to-date and helps the guards maintain control of the prison. In return for their service, these inmates receive "special favors"—cell phones, drugs, and sometimes even weapons. Because many inmates illegally purchase phones and drugs on their own, it's hard to know which of them are in the guards' pockets. Since no one can say for certain who in any instance is talking to the guards, no one can be disciplined for snitching. However, the overall consensus is that "someone" is snitching and sooner or later, often without evidence, an inmate—usually some unfortunate soul who irritated a guard or got on the bad side of a gang member—will be accused as the snitch and suffer the violent consequences.

During the investigation, I was placed in "the hole," an isolation unit where inmates were locked in solitary confinement. The hole is a tremendously lonely place. Most prisons call these facilities either "Isolation Units" or "Administrative Segregation Units," but for inmates it is simply "the hole." My cell was small and dark and because it lacked windows, I sometimes never knew whether it was day or night. The only clues were the guards changing shifts and what kind of meal was served. Some inmates couldn't handle it and broke, yelling and screaming throughout the night. Some went crazy in those cells.

I remained in that hole for months while the county office of the District Attorney was deciding whether to charge me with attempted murder. My only escape was the twice-weekly visits to the small yard for a couple of hours. The guards had found the knife and it looked like an open-and-shut case, but I was never charged. It turned out that because the Sergeant's orders to keep me in my cell that day weren't followed, the safety and security of the prison was potentially compromised, and the Cuban prisoner could have sued the prison for negligence. However, this didn't deter prison officials from imposing their own brand of in-house justice. They found me guilty of stabbing the inmate with a manufactured weapon and sentenced me to an indefinite term at the highest-security unit in the California prison system: San Quentin's Death Row isolation unit north of beautiful San Francisco.

That first year in Soledad was tough enough but San Quentin was an actual nightmare. And you are locked inside the nightmare, with no hope of waking up: long days and long nights alone. Lost and damaged spirits will vent their despair in bone-chilling ways. The screams of some of the men in solitary cells were as horrific as the cries of jungle animals. Even the sane, which I still counted myself among, start to question their own mental states surrounded with such misery. One person who drew particular venom from other inmates in isolation was Charles Manson. He was the cult leader responsible for the 1969 Tate-LaBianca murders. Manson would stay up all night in the hole yelling out obscenities. He would talk about people's heritage and their race. He would scream so loud that it was almost bone shattering. He never came out of his cell to the yard, so no one could get to him. He was in his own little cave and would verbally abuse all of us who were in that building. He was on the tier directly below me. No matter how hard you tried to avoid it, you woke to madness every day. There was no escape. In the hole, a person is held hostage--physically and to the very essence of their soul.

Inmates in San Quentin's Maximum Security Administrative Segregation Unit (ad-seg—their version of "the hole") were allowed eight hours of rec time each week in the yard, at the discretion of the guards, depending on their mood on any given day. Only twenty inmates at a time were allowed on the concrete "yard"—one-fourth the size of a football field without grass or goal posts, only concrete and iron pull-up bars. Instead of loyal fans there were uniformed enforcers with automatic weapons. The cheerleaders were the inmates looking forward to whatever bloodletting might be the order of that day.

I would hear the guard's footsteps walking down the cell block, each iron door clanging open and shut, louder and louder as he approached me. When he finally got to my cell, he'd ask if I was going to the yard. I would always answer

"Yes," desperate for fresh air, but first he'd conduct a "strip search"—a dehumanizing routine of emasculating inmates, common practice in California prisons. Some guards seemed to find great pleasure in it; others were as disgusted as the inmates. I would stand in front of him, separated only by the iron door, and follow his commands. First, I'd strip completely naked. Then I'd show him the inside of my mouth and under my testicles. I'd turn around, bend over, and cough so he could see that nothing was hidden in my rectum. After that I would hand him my clothes, one at a time—pants, shirt, undershirt, socks, shoes, and under-wear—through the partition for dinner trays in the cell door. He would search and return them through the same slot, one at a time, and I would put them back on. After the search, the guard would handcuff me by having me place my hands through the tray slot, then open the door and instruct me to back out. Then I was accompanied to the entrance of the yard where two guards would "wand" me with metal detectors, searching for weapons. They would glide them over my butt, back, shoulders, head, chest, stomach, and groin and then between my legs. Some guards finished by sticking the detector between the inmate's legs from behind which elicited catcalls from inmates calling those guards gay.

Once in the yard, an inmate was free to hang out with whatever group he's comfortable with—or least threatened by. The inmates in this most max of maximum security prisons were considered "the worst of the worst" and they would often attempt to live up (or down) to their billing. Violence was the norm. For example, when an inmate was accused by another inmate of a breach in etiquette or respect, disciplinary measures were always taken. In most cases, the accused wasn't confronted verbally and so had no opportunity to refute the charges—or evade the punishment. Some who know that discipline will be meted out to them will run to the guards for protection, a maneuver known as "locking up" and considered especially cowardly. But punishment was not just reserved for errors in etiquette.

Prison culture is highly structured, and everyone has their place: gang leaders and members; drug dealers, wine (pruno) makers, clerks and other workers; religious guys, and disparate inmates. At the bottom of the hierarchy are cowards, snitches, and child molesters. At some point in their incarceration, each may well have some form of discipline, usually violent, imposed on them. The coward, who hasn't asked for protection, may get beaten once a week. The snitch will get stabbed and child molesters have an extremely low probability of staying alive.

Although guards are mandated by law to protect prisoners, those who aren't part of a gang or another support group must find their own ways to care for themselves. That's the reality of prison life. My chilling introduction to the brutality of the worst prison in California began on my very first day in the yard.

I was watching an inmate use electric hair clippers to cut another inmate's hair. It surprised me, given the lengths guards went through to screen inmates for any metal that could be used as a weapon, but in this particular hole, electric hair clippers were allowed for one inmate—the designated barber. I asked the barber if he could trim my beard after he finished with the other inmate. "Sure," he said. "It'll cost you two Top Ramen soups." He was quick and before I knew it I was wiping the excess hair off my chest and shoulders. Suddenly an officer yelled, "Get down!" simultaneously firing his automatic rifle. When this happens, the rule is to immediately drop face-down on the ground. Those who don't, are assumed to be involved in whatever incident has been observed and could be charged with a violation or even shot. I got down and tried to see what was happening. The inmate barber who had just clipped my beard was rolling on the ground; another inmate was thrashing nearby, blood gushing between his fingers which were held firmly against his head trying to staunch his bleeding. The barber, I noticed, was trying to drop a metal shank down a nearby drain. The guard yelled "Stop!" again and fired his gun. Guards ran onto the yard and handcuffed the barber; other guards milled around as medical personnel placed the injured inmate on a stretcher. The sight of all that fresh blood should have caused more commotion than it did, but little was said or done. The blood was just "business as usual." The guy who got stabbed had been disciplined; the inmate barber had been chosen to deliver it.

One of the many unspoken rules in prison is to mind your own business. An inmate named Wiz told me this and I never forgot the way he put it. "The best business is to have some business of your own," he said. "But if you have no business, make it your business to leave other folks' business alone." This meant not stopping to stare at a fight or observe an argument. Glimpse it, make sure it's not a threat to you, and then keep moving.

After the stretcher left the yard, some of the guards approached each inmate and, in the cold open air, conducted strip searches—under the watchful eyes of the other guards and inmates. When my turn came, I screwed up. Instead of turning around, bending over, squatting, and then coughing, I forgot to squat. I had to do the entire procedure all over again. I was embarrassed, not because I was stark naked in front of a bunch of criminally-minded strangers but because I had made a rookie mistake in front of everyone, in a place where missing protocols or a detail could mean life or death. The crisp air did little to stop the perspiration from rolling down my face.

After all the inmates were stripped and searched, we were individually escorted back to our cells. The walk back to the cells was slow and the silence deafening. No one said anything, not even the guards. Even in a place dominated by instincts for survival, the rawness of violence still brought the specter of mortality uncomfortably close.

When I got back to my cell, I immediately knelt down and prayed, thanking God that I hadn't been the barber's victim and berating myself for being so naïve as to put my throat in the hands of a killer. I stayed on my knees for a very long time, trying to grasp something that felt like a thread of sanity. I was lonely, having no one to talk to about the events of that day. It was day one for me in that prison yard. How was I going to get through this alive?

Later, I learned that it was customary for the prison administration to conduct a ten-day investigation of any incident on the yard, and inmates would not be allowed to return until it was completed. Each investigation took exactly ten days, no matter what had occurred. Once allowed back in the yard, it was business as usual. Some inmate would inevitably "need" discipline; one or two others would be ordered to carry it out. This scenario repeated itself too often: someone gets hurt, a guard shoots, a stretcher appears, a strip search, and then a ten–day lockdown. The only thing that changed were the identities of the victims and enforcers.

The end of a lockdown was an especially dangerous time: the beginning of a period of revenge. A lot can happen in ten days, even when the population is confined to their cells. Ten days were enough time for someone to offend another prisoner, perhaps talking too loudly or some expression of perceived disrespect. All forms of communication with gang members, for example, had to be innocuous, especially if you weren't one of them. The margins of error were very narrow. I wasn't a gang member and therefore, considered "non-affiliated," making me more vulnerable and a potentially easy target. And so, I lived with the understanding that one day I could be next. After each ten-day lockdown, I would debate whether or not to return to the yard. My dread was so palpable and the culture of violence so overwhelming, I couldn't escape the anxiety. It began when lockdown began. I'd wake up every day in a sweat of indecision: Should I choose the yard and its risks of violence hoping for the best? or "lock up," choose the fate of a coward—the only option for those who couldn't cope with the yard's tensions. I would only have to point out some gang or gang member and declare that they'd threatened to hurt me. The guards would then be mandated by law to remove me from the yard or risk a lawsuit if something happened to me after they'd been informed of such a threat. The downside with that choice was that my name would become dirt and bad news travels fast. Lock-ups could never safely return to the general population of inmates. For me that was never an option.

By the fifth day of a lockdown, my stress levels would bring me to a state of paralysis, made worse by the fact that I had no one to talk to, no caring person to help me sort out my thoughts and feelings. I was alone facing life and death decisions in a pitiless universe. Such massive mental agony takes a toll, and each ten-day block of such suffering felt like it had aged me ten years.

Every tenth day, the normal routine would begin again—the guard walking down the tier, stopping at each cell, and calling for the yard. My pulse would race with each approaching step. The closer he got, the weaker and more indecisive I felt. When he finally arrived at my cell, I'd be standing there, mute. Each time, as if the guard intuited my anguish, he'd have me roll up my mattress and take off my clothes, conduct the strip search, and send me down to the yard. It felt as if God or the universe was acting through him, relieving me of the burden of making a decision, but the answer was always the same: The yard was my fate.

They say that familiarity breeds contempt. Over time I became numb to the violence and even experienced a detached anticipation for the next confrontation. But I also feared that I had gone crazy. Such levels of hostility were foreign to me. Violence had always hovered nearby me in the neighborhood where I grew up, but it wasn't in your face daily like it was in the yard. Even worse was when the person being assaulted had become familiar—maybe even almost a friend. One incident in particular has colonized a site in my memory.

Frog had a mean streak—I'd witnessed his brutality on several occasions—but he was also amiable and considered me a friend. I thought this strange because I'd understood that you didn't make "friends" in this place. However, he and I would talk almost every time we were in the yard together. He'd tell me when he was going to beat someone up or when there would be a preplanned attack. I would sometimes send extra food to his cell. Frog was a senior inmate but time in prison ultimately gives no advantage. It didn't matter if you were there for fifteen years or fifteen minutes;

there was no immunity for violating prison etiquette. When you are locked in and become accustomed to an unending cycle of violence and survival, small things easily become big things and someone needs to be blamed for them. No one wanted the finger of responsibility pointed toward them, so people readily found reasons to point the finger at someone else.

Each night before "shut-down" the leader of the most dominant gang recited his pronouncements and gave shout-outs to other gang members who held key positions. These shout-outs are a time-honored tradition of showing respect. After the recitation, the leader would announce that "the program" was over and shut-down would soon begin, which meant that all conversations had to end. This mandate was strongly enforced. It was dangerous to even sneeze too loudly. Everyone had to finish whatever business they had, otherwise they risked being fingered by inmates throughout the five-tiered building who remained alert for any violation.

Frog had made a mistake; he'd mistimed how long it would take him to "fish" for a cigarette. To fish is to throw a makeshift rope (made of a sheet torn into thin strips and tied together) either up or down the tier. Good fishers would attach a flat, weighted object to the front of the rope and swing it back and forth until they achieved enough momentum to fling the line in front of the target cell. The other person would use a makeshift pole made of paper to pull the line into their cell. Once inside, that inmate would attach their own fish line to the "rope" with whatever goods were being exchanged and they would be pulled back to the first cell. The process was fraught with peril. Fish lines frequently broke from overuse on the wet tiers. They could get snagged on the rusty edges of the cell bars or could slide over the edge to another tier. There were no insurance policies for lost or stolen items. First-tier inmates who had "locked up" and knew they were hated anyway and protected only by the guards, would do all they could to snag errant lines and steal the attached goods.

Frog slung his fish line down the tier but it slid off the walkway before Frog could snap it back. A first-tier inmate snagged it at nearly the same moment as the announcement of shut-down. Frog yelled, "Get off my line." The first-tier inmate broke silence and called him a punk bitch.

Frog recognized his error and stopped talking but the first-tier inmate did not, berating Frog, his ancestors, his gang, and his hopeless existence on this earth, throughout most of the night—an egregious violation of etiquette. The gang couldn't discipline the offending inmate because he was locked up and protected, but they could take out their frustrations on someone they had access to, and Frog became the target. Every gang-sanctioned attack had to be justified in some way as necessary and Frog's role in the breach though minimal was clear.

The next morning on the yard, everyone assumed their usual positions, but the stink of fecal matter was in the air, indicating that at least one inmate-manufactured weapon was present—brought to the yard, concealed in a rectum. Everyone in a gang had a job: There were decision-makers, planners, hitters, watchers—and carriers, the lowest in status. Those who couldn't be trusted to make attacks were utilized instead as carriers and were rarely promoted to other duties. They would conceal the weapon, discretely pull it out, wipe it off with toilet paper, and then pass it to the hitter. It was a messy affair, but in the twisted logic of prison life, a necessary one.

Frog came over to me and said he thought they would try to get him today. I told him I didn't know about it, but the signs were clear enough, and I silently hoped that Frog would stay away from me. Unfortunately, Frog had other ideas, believing that if he stayed by me his chances of avoiding trouble would be better. This was poor reasoning. Once an attack had been planned and ordered, it had to be carried out. Otherwise, someone would have to pay the price of failure with their own blood.

Frog was not a little guy; he was strong, and his combat skills were among the best on the yard. It didn't surprise me that two guys were sent to get him. One of them, thin and charcoal black, had a reputation for being the sneakiest, quickest, and most accurate hitter on the yard. They called him Midnight and he was feared. The other hitter was a young guy on Death Row who'd been on the yard for less than a year but had learned quickly. The two of them worked together, stealthily stalking their prey. They started by walking in a circular fashion around the enclosure, passing Frog several times while engaged in seemingly harmless conversation. Frog must have been lulled into a kind of complacency, because after a few trips around the yard, they struck. Midnight was deadly, stabbing Frog in the neck. He fell to the ground, writhing in pain. Some of his blood splattered onto me. The tower guard shot once in my general direction because I was too close to Frog, but I was in shock and couldn't get far enough away. As I prepared to hit the ground, I wiped some of Frog's blood off my face to see where Midnight was—I didn't want to become collateral damage. The guard saw the wiping motion and fired his gun a second time; guards are ordered to fire their weapons at anyone who continues to move after being ordered to stop. The round hit the ground next to my foot and kicked up some of the asphalt, which hit my ankle. I jerked my foot toward my body and he fired a third round. That one was closer to my head. And then I snapped. All sanity left my mind. I had an explosive reaction, no longer caring whether I lived or died—and I stood up. The tower guard fired a fourth round. I could hear the faint sound of inmates yelling for me to get back down. I ran toward the fence and jumped on it, yelling, "Kill me, kill me!" He fired a fifth time. I fell off the fence and hit the ground hard. By this time other guards had responded to the incident and were lined up on the outside of the fence. I got up and jumped back on to the fence. I heard the lieutenant shouting for me to get down. Then a sixth shot. The lieutenant started yelling at the firing guard to lower his weapon. I started climbing off the fence, but the guard couldn't resist taking one last shot.

I know it isn't humanly possible to see a bullet coming toward your head, but I assure you that I saw it, as if in slow motion, coming directly for my right eye. The heat of it passing was unlike anything I'd ever experienced, a rapid, surreal bolt of fire. I fell to the ground and stayed there for what seemed like a very long time, wondering how it would feel to be dead: to be finally done with this yard, this hell, this hopeless life.

The guards came onto the yard in fouler spirits than usual. They rolled me over and checked my body for stab wounds or bullet holes. They cuffed me and escorted me to the lieutenant's office. The lieutenant was tall, tough, smart, and a bit of a psychologist—a mash-up of Jimmy Stewart, John Wayne, Clint Eastwood, and George Clooney. I was placed in a chair staring up at him as he paced around me speaking inaudibly—at least it seemed inaudible; I was in an altered state, unable to focus on what was happening around me. When I was finally able to decipher his words, the first thing that made sense was a question: "Are you crazy or what?" My answer was quick and unmeasured. "This whole world is crazy." He and all the other guards broke out in belly-busting laughter as if that was the funniest thing they'd ever heard. Then there was more conversation, trying to re-establish some normalcy.

The lieutenant flexed his authority by saying he wouldn't charge me with attempted assault on an officer, attempted escape, failing to obey orders, inciting a riot, or stabbing another inmate as long as I stayed out of trouble. He could have charged me and no one would have refuted him, but his goal was intimidation. Furthermore, they also knew that I wasn't involved. The guards took me back to my cell, where I sat alone and motionless the entire night until they slid the breakfast tray through the slot the next morning. We were never told what happened to Frog. I don't know if he lived or died but I never saw him again.

More time went by and I actually became accustomed to life in the hole. The human animal can adapt to almost any-thing, however dire the circumstances. I think of those who survived Auschwitz and Abu Ghraib and other hellholes. What happens to the human spirit and sanity when squeezed and bludgeoned in such crucibles under such conditions? Where's the money to study that? These behaviors are all sanctioned by "civilized" society as retribution for past misdeeds. I believe we humans lose our moral compass when we mistreat or allow the mistreatment of other humans for the sole purpose of punishment or revenge. Treat someone like an animal long enough and they will behave like one; a dog will do as trained. It's really no wonder that the prisoners on that yard—and the guards as well—conducted themselves in such violent ways.

My spontaneous act of rebellion was an act of madness, but it came from a deep place inside my young psyche, overtaxed by the horrid absurdity of it all. From that act came my nickname that stuck: Crazy. Guys would repeatedly recount the story of how I held the record at San Quentin for having been shot at more times than anyone in the prison's history. Sometimes, even the guards would join in the conversation and laughter, amazed that one of their own could shoot that many times and miss. Wizard (an inmate philosopher) would quote the Bible whenever he saw me: "All the arrows of my enemy cannot harm me." When new Death Row inmates came into the yard, the others would take great pleasure introducing me: "This is 'Crazy,' he can't be shot!" The most notorious criminals in California would laugh at, and with, this little guy called Crazy. Sometimes, I would even re-enact the scene while the guards played along. And the story seemed to have a transformative affect. There was less violence on the yard when the inmates were talking and laughing with each other. All because of Crazy's unexpected spasm of crazy.

Every six months or so, a prison administration committee would review an ad-seg inmate's case for staying in the hole, and after seven or eight months, my turn finally arrived. I appeared before the committee with little hope of a favorable outcome. I knew guys who had been in the hole for eleven years. Some were said to be political prisoners, others so violent that they couldn't be trusted in the general prisoner population. The usual conclusion of most committee recommendations was, "Continue present programming; return for review in six months." I entered the committee room in handcuffs and paid little attention to the formalities. Until the committee chairman said, "After looking at your file, I'm wondering if I should take a chance and place you out on the mainline."

I was stunned, not knowing if he was serious or not, but I didn't hesitate to answer him. "Of course, you can take a chance on me," I responded. "I won't let you down."

He said, "I don't want you tearing up my mainline. If you screw up one time, I'll lock you away for so long you'll be an old man before you get out. Is that perfectly clear?" It certainly was.

"Yes sir," I said, and it looked like my days in the hole were finally over.

I entered San Quentin's mainline—the general population—in late 1986. Already well-known as "Crazy," I was immediately greeted by members of different gangs asking about my affiliation. My answer was always the same: "I'm from Chicago!" That short answer, and knowing I came from the hole, was enough to give me an immediate, if temporary, pass.

A few days after my "release" to mainline, I was sitting in the bleachers in the lower yard admiring the size of their recreational space compared to the postage stamp I had just left, when one of the leaders of a well-known African-American gang, the Crips, approached. The Crips leader asked me if I wanted to smoke a joint with him. It would not have been good protocol to refuse, so I took a small hit. Then other members of his gang came over and before I knew it, three joints were being passed around. The crowd grew and the guards noticed, a few of them heading in our direction. The Crips leader asked me to hold onto a fifty-dollar bill as the guards approached and the crowd began to disperse. Again, I was in no position to say no and took it. Even though I knew I was being tested.

There I was, fresh out the hole, alone and high with a fifty-dollar bill in my pocket. As the guards got closer, I became increasingly paranoid. I crumpled the bill into a wad and dropped it between the bleacher seats. The guards walked by and I stepped down, planning to go under the bleacher to get the money, but then they turned around. I headed for the track and noticed that they seemed to be following me. I blended into the traffic of inmates walking around the yard and the guards continued on their way. I kept walking around the track until the high wore off and guys started lining up to leave.

As I was heading toward the line, the Crips leader approached me. He got so close that I could feel his breath on my earlobe. "You got that fifty-dollar bill?" he asked. I was still high, but prior experience had taught me that guys like him didn't want to hear excuses or explanations—they had an image to maintain—so I had to think fast. I pulled him close, put my lips to his ear, and said "Under the bleachers—let's go!" Without hesitation or looking back, we headed there. Once at the bleachers, I saw that a few of his boys had followed us. Again, I got close to him and said that I had dropped the money through the seats.

"Better find it!" he hissed with the same intensity, and we all went under the bleachers to look for that crumpled-up bill. The guard was yelling on the loud speaker to clear the yard. The line was getting shorter and shorter. We couldn't keep looking much longer. He kept asking me, "Where's my fifty?" I knew that if we left the yard without finding it, I would face some nasty consequences. The guard yelled "Final call" on the speaker while other guards were herding stragglers toward the yard gate. The Crips leader and his men left the bleachers and started toward the shrinking line. Perspiration was rolling down my face onto the ground. And then I saw it! I immediately scooped it up and hurried to the line. I pulled him close and placed the money in his hand. "Thanks for having faith in me and trusting me," I whispered. We silently walked into San Quentin's West Block housing unit, and when we arrived at his tier, he said, "See you on the weight pile tomorrow."

I showed up the next day still overwhelmed by the size of the yard. The Death Row yard accommodated about twenty to thirty inmates, but the San Quentin lower yard had room for six hundred. Inmates could choose to run or walk around the track, play basketball, do pull-ups, hit the heavy bag, play dominoes or card games, or work out on the weight pile. That's where I found the Crips. The leader and his crew were already lifting weights and talking smack to each other—but in a spirit of challenging camaraderie. The "target" was supposed to take it from all sides and then deliver his own jabs when the opportunity came. I could tell this was their way of showing affection for each other and it seemed like they could go all day, laughing and wise-cracking. To others it may have seemed abusive, but this was routine, what they were accustomed to, the kind of energy you would find in a close-knit family. To include others in their repartee meant that person was accepted, at least to a point. So, it felt pretty good when I walked up and they greeted me with a hardy "Hey!" or "What's up?"

The Crips leader asked me to do some back arms off the side of the bench with a seventy-five-pound dumbbell. This may have seemed impossible for my compact, 150-pound frame but I'd become pretty strong and decided to give it a try. So, I squatted down, leaning on the side of the bench, slung the dumbbell behind me—and then fell over backwards. Everyone burst out laughing, the other groups on the weight pile joining in. In any normal situation, I would have felt embarrassed, but prison is nowhere close to normal; so I got up, brushed myself off, and laughed along with them.

The next day the Crips leader, his crew, and I walked to the bleachers together. A crowd started to gather, and I found myself telling the story of my time in the hole and of the day I had dodged seven bullets.

They were curious about some of the guys on Death Row: Big Tookie, Raymond Treach, Evil, Sparks, E-man from Watts, and many others. I told them Big Tookie was still big, Treach was still smart, Sparks was solid and quick as ever, and E-man's arms were bigger around than my head! "But don't think of the Hole as a place to hang out with your heroes," I told them. "It's a very lonely place in those musty and dirty cells," I said, "especially late at night."

Talking and laughing with others sure beat fighting, and I found myself relaxing somewhat. I seemed to have a talent for putting others at ease. Then I noticed that the guards were paying closer attention to me after I'd been on the mainline for a few days. They seemed especially interested in the way I spoke with groups of inmates. When one guard accused me of being a gang leader, I responded almost casually, "Sure, if the name of the gang is the human race."

Well, without thinking, I had stepped into a snare. Two days later, I was charged with conspiracy to assault a correctional officer. *Conspiracy to Assault?* It's easy for a guard or a prison administrator to accuse an inmate of a rules violation, since they never have to prove a thing. They'll give the inmate a perfunctory hearing that always boils down to a single question: "Who are you going to believe, a convicted felon or an officer sworn to protect society?" Imagine being captive in a system where you have no legal recourse when you believe the few rights you do have are being trampled. You can't respond in a violent manner because that will cost you more in the long run, and if you try to respond in accordance with the rules, you'll drown in a bottomless pit of paperwork.

Many inmates spend countless hours filing grievances or counter-grievances against guards or administrators, and then, once they've submitted all the necessary documents and waited for a decision—usually many weeks—

someone responds with the simple verdict: "Your claim is without merit." Some inmates tell themselves that the next time will be different, but we all know that doing the same thing over and over again and expecting a different result is the definition of insanity. "Jailhouse lawyers"—inmates who spend hours a day in the law library working on behalf of other inmates—are also used, but the outcome is nearly always the same and they still take an inmate's money or barter. Such unethical practices are not unusual in "normal" society where lawyers knowingly take advantage of their clients' naiveté and ignorance. This certainly happened to me when my court-appointed defense attorney advised me not to take a plea bargain before my second trial, but it's unconscionable for a fellow inmate, who is supposedly your ally, to behave in such a manner. I saw this happen time and again in prison—however well-meaning some of the "jailhouse lawyers" might have been.

After only eight days on the mainline, I was escorted in handcuffs back to the hole. Guys were calling out as I was paraded to my cell, "Crazy is back!"

"I told you he wouldn't last out there."

"He probably stabbed the Warden." The loudest guy yelled, "Hey, Crazy, see you in ten days on the yard."

I had forgotten how mind-shatteringly loud it was in San Quentin's ad-seg and how the smell was overwhelming. If the violence didn't get you, the sensory overload would. I couldn't sleep for two days. I kept berating myself for being so high profile on the mainline. Why didn't I just blend in with the squares or church guys? Why did I link up so visibly with gang members and draw the wrath of the guards like a lightning strike? I knew the answers all too well: I was always looking to be liked and, unfortunately at times, by the wrong people.

Chapter Five

New Folsom Prison Blues

Bᵁᵗ this time, my stay in San Quentin's hole proved to be relatively short. The California prison system had just opened a brand new, taxpayer-funded, "state-of-the-art," Level 4 (maximum security) prison. Its official title was California State Prison, Sacramento (CSP-Sacramento), but it was known as New Folsom because it had been built next to another prison called Old Folsom—the second oldest in California and the subject of Johnny Cash's "Folsom Prison Blues."

Because of serious over-crowding issues across the state prison system, New Folsom wasn't even fully completed before prisoners were forced to move in. A considerable number of inmates in the San Quentin hole who were not on Death Row, which included me, were sent to New Folsom. Inmates from the hole in Old Folsom were also sent to help fill it. Because the new prison was publicly funded, the powers that be determined to open it on schedule despite the fact that it was incomplete. They didn't care about the dangers of throwing the most dangerous inmates from two of the state's most notorious prisons together in one facility. They just wanted to be able to report to the public that the prison was finished on time and fully stocked with inmates.

When we first arrived at New Folsom, an incident occurred that had ramifications the Administration could not have foreseen. The guards had been repeatedly briefed and warned about the "hardest of the hard" inmates arriving at this new prison. They had been told not to take any lip, to do whatever they thought necessary to show them who was boss. And so, they did. When we first got off the bus in shackles, we were taken in single file to an interview room—where we were to be told, one at a time, the rules of New Folsom.

While we were waiting our turns, still in chains, a shot was heard from inside the interview room. The guards started yelling at us to "Get down!" News quickly circulated that an inmate had just been shot in the head. As we lay face down on the ground, we wondered aloud who it was. You could hear members of various gangs whispering to each other: "Was it Blood? Cuz? Comrade?" Everyone wanted to know. We got the answer when a stretcher came out carrying a young Crips gang member. He had been shot through the eye. We were then taken two-by-two to our cells, locked in, and not told the condition of the kid who'd been shot.

The administration tried to spin a story that the inmate had a knife. Unlike most stories that administrators got away with in the past, this one didn't stand in the face of irrefutable contrary evidence. Most damning was the fact that, as procedures dictated, each inmate remained hand-cuffed during the entire interview process. The attorneys for the family of the prisoner who had been shot questioned how he could have escaped his handcuffs and pulled out a knife under the watchful eyes of the guards. Houdini would have had trouble pulling that one off, let alone a young gangster from southeast Los Angeles.

The prison administration ultimately folded and paid the family a settlement. It came, of course, with a non-disclosure agreement, preventing the family and their lawyer from speaking publicly about the incident. Normally, when it comes to prisons, the public cares little about anything besides misappropriation of taxpayer funds or being "too easy" on inmates. However, hearing that a young hand-cuffed man had been shot in the head might provoke even the most uncaring citizen to pause and question their state's prison system.

Nevertheless, despite the settlement, the guards' intent to demonstrate that they were the baddest gang in the prison, had a chilling effect on inmate life.

Meanwhile, we were locked down. The problem was, New Folsom was "stocked" with inmates but hardly finished. Debris and large rocks from unfinished construction were strewn about in what was to be the recreational yard. The guards' union demanded that the prison be locked down for six months while the materials were removed. This meant that for those six months we were locked in our cells twenty-four hours a day. During that period, guards would release a few inmates to sweep the tiers. When food arrived from the dining hall, those same inmates passed the trays through door slots into the cells. The inmates selected to work on the tiers—"tier runners"—were chosen according to their ethnicity—Black, Latino or "white." There had to be an equal representation of each race to avoid charges of special treatment or racism. The position was coveted since tier runners were given privileges: extra food from the dining hall; longer showers. They could loiter on the tiers until the next shift of officers came on duty. New officers could select their own tier runners for their shift, but often they would use the runners from the earlier shift.

Tier runners were important to both the guards and other inmates. If an inmate called out, "I need a runner on the back bar of the second tier," it could be anything from delivering a newspaper from one inmate to another to something deadlier, such as transferring a weapon to a carrier. The practice of "fishing" was made obsolete by these runners. Tier runners were primarily attached to their own ethnic group; they could service other races but only on a very limited basis. An African-American tier runner would not be expected to stop at a Caucasian cell and a Caucasian runner wouldn't be caught dead (so to speak) at an African-American cell.

Finally, after six months of lockdown, the rocks and construction debris were removed, and prison administrators gave the order to release inmates to the recreational yard. Of course, when the six- month lock-down finally ended, it didn't take a Nostradamus to predict what would happen next. To forgive may be divine, but nothing is ever forgotten or forgiven in prison.

Having full understanding that inmates had been locked in their cells for the better part of six months, prison staff believed they were prepared for whatever might ensue. They assumed that if they kept the inmates fighting against one another, they would maintain control of the prison. What they couldn't prepare for was the level of inmates' wrath against the guards.

Led by leaders of the Crips—whose young member had been shot in the eye six months earlier—inmates from several gangs coordinated to carry out simultaneous attacks on the guards. Of course, like Native Americans charging the fully loaded guns of the U.S. Cavalry with bows and arrows, many inmates were hurt and only one guard was seriously injured. Ironically, he oversaw the prison bakery and was one of the few well-liked guards known to place extra cookies on trays while we were locked down. He had a wild laugh and always seemed to be in a good mood. He wasn't intimidated by the "inmate lover" tag that guards would hurl at their colleagues who treated inmates with some semblance of humanity. Unfortunately, the inmates who attacked him didn't know him; they were just "following orders."

The administration's response to the violence followed a predictable course. Total lockdown was immediately reinstated. After an investigation, critical inmate workers who were not members of the ethnic group or gang involved in the incident were allowed to return to their jobs to keep the prison functioning by working in the kitchen and laundry. A few days after that, inmates from the general population who were not members of gangs connected to the incident were released to the rec yard. Inmates involved in the violence would remain in lockdown for however long administrators wanted to keep them there.

During lockdowns, prisons receive extra money to compensate for "hazardous conditions" and guards make higher pay for emergency overtime. This incentivizes keeping some segment of the prison population locked down in order to keep the cash flowing in. Prisons also receive more money for operating at maximum capacity, which means that officials will find creative methods to keep every prison bed occupied. It was common practice for California Department of Corrections and Rehabilitation (CDCR) to move inmates between prisons to ensure the right numbers to maximize funding. Transportation expenses is a very easy way to increase the cost of operating a prison in a very short time.

One learns quickly that the business of prisons is not concerned with morality or justice. It's about money. It is no coincidence that, since the opening of New Folsom and other prisons in the eighties and nineties, the percentage of California's taxpayer funded budget dedicated to its prison system has increased astronomically. Driving that increase are staff paychecks, facilitated by the guard union's influence on politics in the state capitol.

In 2011, Governor Jerry Brown attempted to address some of these issues, emphasizing at the start of his campaign that he would not be bought off by special interests. To the guard's union, this was a coded warning that their tax-funded party was about to end—no more vacation homes, sports cars, boats, or motorcycles. No more nepotism. No more publicity billboards advertising how they walked the "toughest beat in California."

The union mounted a fierce counter attack, enlisting their traditional allies—the California District Attorneys Association and specific victim's rights groups tossing money around like confetti. In the end, Governor Brown managed to reduce the number of inmates in state prisons by transferring many nonviolent felons to county jails. This reduced the influence of the guards' union while giving more power to county sheriffs.

But while I was at New Folsom all these reforms were still in the future. And so, after the yard opening-uprising, the prison went back on lockdown. But the violence didn't stop. It seemed as if guards and inmates alike were revising their strategies and plans. During this time, drugs began appearing in larger amounts inside. It doesn't take a rocket scientist to deduce where those drugs were coming from. Special guards known as Gang Coordinators walked the yard and "jacked up" (searched) certain inmates to make it appear they were harassing them. It was a transparent ploy.

The guards used those searches to trade drugs for information and influence. Those inmates could then disperse some of the drugs to their gang lieutenants who would distribute smaller portions to their soldiers. The gang with the most drugs would usually have the most members. In prison, a person could buy almost anything with drugs: extra food, clean clothing, the best cell, even a lover. This is how loyalty was bought and paid for, and control secured by the guards.

The introduction of drugs into the prison accomplished several important things. First, controlling the access kept power in the guards' hands. It also fostered animosity and competition between gangs and even members of the same gang. Jealousy and greed inevitably caused gang leaders to plot against each other, once blood was shed, there would never be peace, only retaliation.

Prison officials were Machiavellian at dividing and conquering. With information provided by their informants, Gang Coordinators could orchestrate tensions between gangs the way a good director utilizes actors. They would be pre-supplied with up-to-date information on all new arrivals and their gang affiliations. They would know in advance when one gang was planning to attack another gang. This tactic was a parallel system to the technique gang leaders used in the yard at San Quentin when inmates "knew" when someone would be attacked.

Gang Coordinators walked the yard as untouchables. If an inmate looked at them sideways, that inmate would for inexplicable reasons find himself in conflict with some gang member. The relationship worked both ways. If a man has sculpted his body to perfection, or is a "pretty" youth, it's no stretch of imagination to see why female guards and even some male guards might find a way to "trade favors."

A Gang Coordinator's favorite inmate could demean even guards in public and those guards were helpless to respond because they knew that inmate was the Gang Coordinator's "boy." This happened often.

Few Californians fully appreciate the day to day life inside prison. Most wouldn't have a clue that some inmates walk around the prison with seemingly more power than some guards wield. The ordinary citizen would probably be most surprised to learn that the majority of drugs within the prison are brought in by guards. It is obvious that prisons are built to be out of sight and out of mind. Californians are expected simply to trust that prisons are operated humanely and that they in fact make our society safer. The high recidivism rate should indicate the failure of such misguided faith in the prison system. As a person who has lived through decades inside the walls of many prisons in California and has seen abuses that have taken place within those walls, I know that faith is misdirected. I experienced the California prison system in all its ugliness and I did it mostly with a clear and observant mind.

I didn't use drugs and wasn't part of a gang at New Folsom. I did, however, need money. Even though I was far from the out-of-shape "doughboy" I had once been, I still loved to eat.

Prison food was comparable to gruel so I needed to buy food directly from the kitchen workers and prepare it myself. Jobs with the Prison Industry Authority (PIA) paid the most of all prison jobs, but an inmate had to work at one of those jobs a long time before the pay came anywhere close to what I needed.

At the time, an inmate sweeping and mopping the tier made about nineteen cents an hour. In 1988, I went to work for the PIA and was immediately put on the laundry shift sorting through dirty clothing. You can imagine how rewarding that work was, so I searched all the other areas within the laundry department and decided I wanted to work with the finished product—clean laundry. However, in prison, inmates don't get to choose what they want or don't want. In the case of the PIA, you had to put in your time to acquire any leverage.

I started observing the inmate lead-man of the distribution section closely and after a few days told him I was very good with numbers and could count up the laundry carts and reconcile them with a bill of lading that I would prepare for him. That would save him some work, so he went to his "free staff" supervisor (a civilian employee working for the prison and not a guard), with whom he had a "symbiotic" relationship. Soon I was switched from the soil/sort section to the distribution section where I then implemented an accounting system for all the laundry-cleaning contracts for State Agencies, departments and institutions like Napa State hospital that the PIA's facility at New Folsom was fulfilling.

Of course, the lead-man took credit for my work, but he got me a raise to forty cents an hour for an eight-hour shift. The money was better than the guys who swept and mopped the cell block tiers but still wasn't enough to sufficiently upgrade my food options.

I had quickly figured out the distribution system and the supervisor became aware of my work ethic and appreciated my (long-neglected) math smarts. When the inmate lead-man found himself on the losing end of a yard fight and was taken to the hole, the supervisor needed a new inmate to fill the position. He submitted my name but ran into a problem with the PIA Superintendent (also free staff) who didn't think I'd worked in the laundry long enough to be promoted. I asked if I could speak with the Superintendent myself and a meeting was arranged.

I entered the Superintendent's big office and sat down. He was short and wide with a raspy voice as if he'd been shouting his entire life. "I make it a practice of promoting inmates according to how much time they've worked on the job," he said, getting right to the point. "That makes sense," I replied, "but it doesn't take into consideration the value that someone newer might be contributing to your bottom line." I knew that because of all the violence and lock-downs that he could never guarantee that state contracts would be fulfilled on time.

"What if the violence in the laundry ceased?" I asked.

"If that happened," he said, "it would change everything."

I was ready for this moment and told him I could implement a system that would guarantee no violence—inmates working and fulfilling contracts.

"I don't believe you can do all that," he said.

Undeterred, I pressed on. "Give me the lead-man job, allow me to place certain inmates in key positions with commensurate pay increases, and I guarantee I will accomplish what I've said." I added that this would only cost the PIA a few extra pennies a month in exchange for making thousands of dollars in completed contracts.

He said he still wasn't convinced that I could do what I said.

I was ready for this moment too. "Okay, give me a probationary period. After ninety days, if there's been no violence and we're getting the clothes out, then you make me the lead-man and pay me and the inmates I select wages commensurate with the promoted positions."

He looked away and scratched his fleshy chin. "So, we give you interim tags only and no pay increases until after ninety days?"

I nodded.

"And there won't be any violence?"

I said, "No. None!"

"And all the contracts will be fulfilled?" Yes.

"All right," he said, adding ominously that if it didn't happen, I wouldn't be working in the laundry anymore—or worse.

I returned to my cell and began formulating my plan. I knew from the revolutionary teachings of my former cellmate, Russell from Soledad, that violence and threats of violence always resulted in more governmental presence. Russell used to say that citizens were fooled into thinking that repression by government was necessary for order. But (he always added) the philosophies of laissez-faire and John Locke taught that people will secure such order in their own self-interest if they can learn to trust and feel they can benefit from cooperation.

True of prison inmates as well? We would see!

The next morning, I went to work early and arranged chairs in the back of the laundry. I had assembled a list of inmates whom I considered good candidates and asked them to show up. It included certain leaders from different gangs and inmates who would be most influential in helping me accomplish my mission. In the meeting, I was clear and matter-of-fact. I said if we can agree that the laundry would be considered off limits for any violence, just like the church and the visiting room, then we could all get more money much faster than the normal waiting period. If we could finish a certain number of pounds of clothing each day, we could keep our new positions and get raises for those positions after ninety days. The eventual raises would range from sixty cents an hour for them to ninety cents an hour for me—near the top of the inmate pay scale.

An inmate named Red Dog wanted to know how I could promise that we all would get pay raises. He was tall with a chiseled body and a scarred face that gave the impression of a serious danger. He held considerable rank and respect within his gang. I knew that if I could convince Red Dog, his loyal soldiers would follow.

I had my answers ready. I said I had made a deal with the Superintendent. Red Dog scoffed. "You think that fat son-of-a-bitch is going to keep his word?" I said he would. "Man, I hope you ain't playin' us for punks," he said. I explained that the superintendent will look good to his PIA bosses because all the contracts will be filled—and he won't dare jeopardize that once everything gets rolling smoothly. After more questions and answers, we all agreed that we were going to make this work and reap the benefits. One of Red Dog's boys wanted to light a joint in celebration of our agreement and anticipated new wealth. I reminded him that we wouldn't actually get the raises for three months. He lit the joint anyway.

I was now the inmate boss. "Wish me luck, Russell," I whispered to my long-ago mentor.

I placed eight inmates in key positions in the laundry department, now regarded as a violence-free zone. Once the gangs had all agreed to this policy, no one dared to violate it. (At that time in California, there were six major prison gangs: Crips, Bloods, Black Guerrilla Family, Mexican Mafia, Northern Familia, and the Aryan Brotherhood.) If anyone broke ranks on the agreement, they would no longer be safe in the general population. If you had a beef with someone, you took care of it outside the laundry. I talked the superintendent into requesting that the associate warden designate laundry workers as critical workers who would be allowed to work even if the prison was on lock down. They agreed, and the pieces of my plan started falling into place.

We began to get the clothing done on a regular schedule. Each section knew how much work it needed to accomplish each day. We were fulfilling the contracts and there was zero violence. The weeks went by and I was counting the days before our positions became permanent and we received our pay raises. I had already calculated how much food I could buy each week. Everything was working out as I had anticipated.

When the three-month probation ended, I went to the superintendent's office. His clerk told me he couldn't see me today and that I should come by the office tomorrow. The next day, the clerk said the superintendent was in a meeting. The day after that, the superintendent was out of the office again. On Friday, I stayed in front of the office all day until the superintendent finally called me in. He said that he'd spoken with his boss at the PIA who told him he couldn't pay out any raises that quarter. I remembered the words of Red Dog: "You think that fat son-of-a-bitch is going to keep his word?" The superintendent assured me that we would receive the raises in three more months. I said we'd agreed that the raises would happen at the end of these three months. I reiterated that the contracts were being fulfilled and that there had been no violence. He said he understood but it was out of his hands.

I walked out of his office completely dejected, struggling to breathe and feeling like I had a rope around my neck. The prison system's lack of integrity was crushing. I went to the loading dock and sat at the end of the ramp. A few inmates came over to me and asked what was wrong. I said I needed to speak with certain inmates and they put out the word. The laundry crew showed up and listened to what I had to say. I said we kept our part of the agreement, but the superintendent would not honor it. Red Dog grunted an "I told you so." I said there has to be a way to get his attention and make him understand that, in prison, all a man has is his word. I needed time to think. Everyone walked away. I felt an arm around my shoulder. It was Red Dog's boy handing me a joint.

Soon after returning to the laundry room, the scream of the alarm shattered our routine and overwhelmed the noise of the big industrial washers and dryers. It was so loud I felt as if my brain was cracking. I got face down on the ground. The guards let it ring for what seemed like an eternity. I knew that sound all too well, but it hadn't rung in the laundry for quite some time and the intensity of it was unbearable. The laundry immediately filled with guards. A stretcher came rolling fast from the back and I could tell by the cowboy boots who was on it: the free-staff supervisor from my section. There was blood on his shirt. Maybe he was in the wrong place at the wrong time. They rushed him out and kept us on the ground for hours. They finally brought an inmate out from the back in handcuffs. He was yelling something inaudible.

The lieutenant ordered interviews of everyone in the laundry and threatened to lock down everyone until he found out exactly what happened and why. By the time my turn came, he already had the whole story. He said, "I hear all the inmates down here are pissed off because they've been working for free. What do you know about that?" I said that I didn't know anything, that one minute I was working and the next minute I was on the floor face down on top of a pile of laundry. The lieutenant leaned toward me in his chair. "You all better pray that the free-staff survives that attack." I felt sick.

Next, I was then taken to the laundry Superintendent's office. The Associate Warden was sitting in the big chair inside that big office. He said that the superintendent had told him that the raises had been approved and we would see our increase this pay period. We were all escorted back to our cells. I lay on my mattress and wondered why it took an act of aggression to convince someone to just do the right thing; why some people respond only to violence instead of kindness. I could only guess that the Superintendent felt he could get away with not paying us, but when his cash cow was threatened, he realized his miscalculation. Facilitating our raises was hardly an act of contrition—more like reacting to a cold slap from reality.

The next day we returned to the PIA laundry and heard that the injured free staff was recuperating. I was most grateful for that. He likely had nothing to do with the events leading up to the incident. We were never told what happened to his assailant, though. I can only assume he met some kind of bad end. And I never found out who ordered the hit and why. Nevertheless, we'd received our raises, were fulfilling contracts, and the business of the laundry continued. Days and weeks passed without much change. Unlike New Folsom's mainline, the laundry remained a violence-free zone upheld by the inmates, not the guards, and we were always released early after a lockdown.

Even with all the accomplishments, it still seemed as if my life was very solitary and lonely. I felt good about our achievement, but it felt like a foxhole in the middle of a war. Whenever I left it, I re-entered a world of danger and unpredictability. How does one make peace with that?

Chapter Six

Helping Hands

Not long after I arrived at New Folsom in 1987, I had requested a transfer to the California Medical Facility (CMF) in Vacaville. It had a therapy program for prisoners who had been in the hole for long stretches, and I still felt scarred from that experience of isolation. These requests were usually denied except in very unusual circumstances. However, in the spring of 1989, I was called to the counselor's office. He informed me that my request to enter the CMF therapy program had been granted.

I was surprised because I had almost forgotten about it. Since I was doing such a good job in New Folsom's laundry—which had been noticed by the Associate Warden—I didn't think I had a chance to be transferred; prisons, as a matter of convenience, keep inmates who are useful. But none of that mattered now. When a request is granted, a prisoner has to comply.

I had made many acquaintances at New Folsom—relationships that were deeper than mere recognition, and I had mixed feelings about leaving. On the one hand, I knew the guys in the laundry counted on me and my leadership and some of them had almost become friends. On the other, New Folsom was the second highest security prison in California, surpassed only by the hole and Death Row in San Quentin. To leave such a volatile place would be a huge relief.

I arrived at CMF and was immediately taken to a secure section of the housing unit that was sectioned off by a metal gate. Another "hole." I could see the general population of inmates on the other side and they could see me. Of course, they wondered who the new guy was. A few of them yelled questions.

"Hey, what's your name?"

"Where did you come from?"

"Do you need any smokes"?

No smokes, thanks, and I told them my name was James—realizing that it was time to leave "Crazy" and his reputation behind forever. I was happy to be just the "new guy." Other inmates who were locked behind that gate as well called out from their cells, telling me what the routine would be. Dinner would be brought on a tray. I'd be allowed to shower in the morning. I would also be taken to the prison's Classification Committee. And sure enough, everything happened as they described it, almost to the letter. In the committee meeting, the Captain said that he was concerned that I wouldn't fit in at CMF. "Looking at your record," he said, "where you've been and what you've done, you may not be able to adjust in a positive manner."

I assured the committee that I wanted to take the therapy program and that I wouldn't cause anyone any trouble. I was told that since this was a lower-level facility, my movements throughout the prison would be limited and monitored for a period of time. I would be allowed to leave my cell during the day to participate in the program but would have to return at three o'clock. I made it my personal mission to get along with everyone and do well in the program.

I was placed in a group with about ten other inmates. We were all serving term-to-life sentences, which meant none of us knew when, or if, we would ever be released from prison. Our group was called "The Lifers"— prisoners without established parole release dates. Most of the men in the group were older than me and many were born in California. Some were former gang members who had "heavy" reputations throughout the prison system. Many had been in prison far longer than me. Most were African-American.

The psychiatrist who ran the group talked very slowly and looked as though he was half asleep, but when he did say something, he spoke with a certain level of wisdom. He admonished us to control ourselves no matter what was occurring around us, emphasizing that if we couldn't control ourselves, someone else would. I came to enjoy that group. I was most impressed by the stories the guys would tell. One in particular that got my attention concerned what prison was like prior to all the new recruits (guards) being hired as the system expanded. Years earlier, guards had treated their work as more of a job and inmates more like workers. Everyone had a task to perform and as long as they did, things went more or less smoothly. Now however, the new guards approached their work as an obligation to make prisoners suffer. They carried an attitude of superiority, implying that inmates weren't their equal as human beings. It was the same attitude that inner city police manifest, which makes it easier for them to justify their brutality toward criminals or even suspects. There was much discussion in the group about the number of prisons and the relentless construction of new ones. This was during the time that California's prison system was expanding to accommodate both an influx of new prisoners and also those who were caught in the rising tide of recidivism. The parole system had been tightened and the "war on drugs" had netted a huge population of nonviolent criminals, packing prisons to the rafters. Even so, the psychiatrist kept stressing the notion that we could not afford to let these changing circumstances derail whatever progress we were making.

A few months later, the psychiatrist announced that the therapy program at CMF was being discontinued, leaving us in a state of dismay. We had all assumed—or hoped—that it would go on indefinitely and had come to rely on it as a reminder of our humanity. He said that a similar program was underway at the California Men's Colony (CMC) in San Luis Obispo. He wouldn't be part of it but said we were welcome to apply for acceptance. I was faced with the very real possibility of being transferred back to the violent, high-security world of New Folsom, the thought of which rattled me to the bone. I had gotten comfortable with prison life at CMF. There was more freedom and less tension. CMC would be a further improvement. It too was a lower-security prison and because it wasn't a medical facility, it offered more educational and vocational programs than any other prison. I believed I could do well at CMC.

I went to my counselor and requested a transfer there to continue my therapy. He seemed amused that I thought I could qualify. He reminded me that my recent stays at higher-security institutions were enough to make me be regarded as a dangerous risk. I asked him if it was the decision of the sending facility or CMC whether or not I would be accepted. He said the decision was CMC's.

I responded that the program at CMF was helping me tremendously and I was serious about continuing on that positive path. I asked him if he would recommend a transfer. He said he would … think about it.

Three months later I was called before the classification committee again. This time the hearing lasted just a few minutes. The committee chairperson said, "We are transferring you to CMC to continue your therapy." Either all my hard work and effort had been noticed by the powers-that-be, or a higher power must have responded to my pleas.

As soon as I stepped off the bus at CMC, I was ushered directly to the hole. I was shocked and asked every guard I encountered why I'd been put there. The answer was always the same: "You tell me." It was as if the sins of my past would never release me. For every break that came my way, there another obstacle appeared.

Sitting on my bunk feeling sorry for myself, I heard someone on the tier. I got up and stood at my cell bars. I saw an inmate porter whistling while he swept. When he saw me, he said, "Hey, I know you from Soledad. You're the guy who stabbed that Cuban dude."

"That was a long time ago," I said.

"You're still in the hole for that?"

"I really don't know why I'm here," I said, miserably.

"Let me find out. I'll talk to Captain Jones about it. He was at Soledad when we were there."

"Okay," I said, with a glimmer of hope. "Thanks." He went back to sweeping the tier.

The evening passed and as I sat on my bunk, I kept wondering if the porter would really talk to the captain. In prison, inmates don't just approach captains for casual conversation. With every passing moment, I chided myself for believing that this porter would actually question a captain about why I was in the hole. I went to sleep that night wondering how soon it would be before I woke up again in New Folsom.

The next morning, I found a document on the floor of my cell which read in part, "This inmate has a proclivity toward weapons and violence. This inmate is deemed to be a threat to the safety and security of this institution." I was heartbroken. My hopes that CMC might be a new opportunity to continue my growth were dashed. After another night of fitful sleep, I sat on my bunk most of the morning wallowing in self-pity. Early that afternoon I heard steps approaching. These were not the regular shuffle of a tier-tending inmate or the crisp tattoo of a shift-walking guard. They were the steps of someone with authority, steps I could recognize after nearly seven years of incarceration.

I got off my bunk and walked to the cell bars. A moment later a uniformed man stopped at my cell. It was the captain. "I heard you wanted to speak with me," he said very sternly. "Yes sir!" I said. "I got off the bus from CMF and was taken straight to this hole."

"I know," he said, and waited.

I nervously went on. "I am not a threat to anyone. I just want the opportunity to do well. You don't have to worry about me. I will get along with everyone. I just want a chance."

"Why should I allow you on my yard and put my bars on the line?" he replied. I looked at the bars on his collar and said, "Because you will look back at your decision and say it was one of the best you ever made as a captain." He looked me in the eye and said, "I can't promise you anything, but I'll look into it." As he walked away, his steps seemed even more authoritative than when he came.

The next morning, I was told to dress for classification. I was taken in handcuffs to the committee. I sat before the chairperson, a lieutenant, a sergeant, and the correctional counselor who wrote the document stating that I had a proclivity toward weapons and violence. The chairperson said, "We're releasing you to the general population, but if we get even one complaint from an officer about you, you will be on the first bus out of here. Is that clear?" I said, "Yes sir!" I had a new lease on life. I knew I would do well with it. And I did.

I sent a letter to my brother informing him that I was at a new prison which was much better than any other prison I'd been too. I enclosed a visitor's form for him to fill out. I even sent a hopeful letter to my long-suffering mother.

Then I wrote to my Aunt Sybil, my father's oldest sister who lived in Brooklyn, New York. Though I had never met her in person, she had become an integral part of my life on the inside. From the time my father died in 1984 and throughout my prison time, my Aunt Sybil and I corresponded by mail and phone calls. She had no children of her own and had very generously taken me under her wing. She was well-educated and had moved from Arkansas more than 40 years ago. Now a feisty New Yorker, her understanding and sense of humor had helped me through some of the bleakest moments in my prison journey.

I explained to Aunt Sybil that I had been sent to this special prison that offered lots of educational opportunities. I told her that I was eager to take advantage of them but that it would require a full-time commitment and I wouldn't be able to work in a prison job. She asked how much I could make at a prison job and I told her about $30 a month sweeping the floor. She said she'd be happy to help and could send me $50 a month so I could concentrate on my studies.

With the security of her support I enrolled in groups, vocational classes, and a college program. I received "A's" in every class and began risking hope because everything was moving in a positive direction.

For the first time since I'd been imprisoned I was allowed to be out after dark, where in a moment of extreme joy, I saw the moon for the first time in seven years. I felt as though I had stumbled out of a cave and seen sunlight for the first time.

In 1992, after two years at CMC and nine years of incarceration, I was scheduled for my first parole board hearing. I felt optimistic. I had done everything right. I had an unblemished disciplinary record. I was more than ready to rejoin the outside world.

People convicted of first- or second-degree murder with the possibility of parole are eligible for a hearing to determine their suitability for release after serving about two-thirds of their sentence. For first-degree murder (25 years-to-life) it's 16 years and 9 months; for second-degree murder (15 years-to-life) it's 9 years and 9 months. The official purpose of these hearings is for the Parole Board to decide whether or not an inmate is still a threat to society. In theory, the Board arrives at their decision by reviewing the record of the crime, the institutional behavior of the prisoner, and the prisoner's plans for after he gets out. In the vast majority of cases, the Board concludes that the prisoner "remains a threat to society" and routinely denies parole requests, almost never letting someone out on their first appearance. Even though these hearings are mandated by law to give inmates the opportunity to plead for their release, the usual outcome is to keep them incarcerated.

As one might imagine, justice is not always served by these hearings and politics plays a huge role. At the time of my first hearing, a conservative governor wanting to appear tough on crime had appointed parole board commissioners whose stance on crime and punishment paralleled his. Most were former law enforcement officials who believed in locking people up and keeping them there. Most were white, male, conservative, and middle class—hardly a panel of my peers. They knew a lot about incarceration but very little about humanity and potential for change, routinely dismissing the possibilities of redemption and forgiveness. Many would no doubt claim to be Christian but conveniently overlook parts of the Bible demonstrating Jesus's compassion: "I needed clothes and you clothed me; I was sick, and you looked after me; I was in prison and you came to visit me."

The racial and demographic composition of the California Parole Board has been grounds for several lawsuits, and abuses of the board are well-documented in California

Court cases. Most common have been claims that its composition never represents the inmates who sit before it. Civilians and working class, multi-racial peers might bring a more humane perspective. Some lawsuits have been filed by jailhouse lawyers, often for violations of liberty and abuse of authority. The liberty issue is very clear: A prisoner has what is legally called a "liberty interest" in freedom. If the Board denies this liberty without good cause, it becomes a legitimate legal issue. Of course, these jailhouse lawyers have neither the resources nor judicial connections of state attorney generals and their deputy attorneys. Not surprisingly, the vast majority of prisoner-initiated lawsuits are summarily denied by the Courts as without merit.

Even in cases where a prisoner's parole is granted, the final outcome remains in doubt. In 1988 California gave its governors the authority to reverse decisions of the Parole Board within five months, and they have used that authority far more often than not. Both Democratic Governor Gray Davis and Republican Governor Arnold Schwarzenegger reversed Parole Board releases approximately 80% of the time. Given that the Board only ever grants a tiny percentage of releases and that those "law and order" governors deny 80% of them, the system is clearly rigged to keep people in prison once they arrive there.

And so there I was, standing before the Parole Board in 1992 for my first hearing. I had served approximately nine years of my 15-to-life sentence. Even knowing what I did about the parole system, I believed against all reason that I would be given a release date. I had diligently prepared for the hearing and asked each of my instructors, supervisors, and even floor-level correctional officers to write a recommendation for me. Maybe one in ten actually did, most likely assuming that their letter wouldn't make a difference, and they were right.

Despite all my efforts and history of good behavior, the Board denied my request and suggested that I accomplish certain goals before my next appearance, which they set for 1994, two years later. I was heartbroken. I felt I had already accomplished those "certain goals" and believed I was ready to re-enter society. As I walked out of that hearing and back across the prison yard to my cell, I felt as if I had just been sentenced to two more years of hard labor. Over those next two years I accomplished everything the Board had asked and more. I earned an Associate of Arts degree in General Education and completed my State Licensing as an X-Ray Technician. It was heavy lifting. While most inmates did time in the rec yard building their muscles, I was committed to building my mind—not unlike my days as a kid in Chicago. Learning everything I could fulfilled my purpose: to become the best person I could be. I started feeling human again. It wasn't enough that I wanted to learn all I could; I wanted to get all "A's." I felt great whenever my hard work was rewarded with the highest marks. Also, receiving high marks in the vocational course of X-ray technology made me believe I could achieve anything— even a post-prison life and career.

Over the next two years I lined up job offers and a place to live in the community. I had more letters from the prison staff attesting to the person I'd become. All of these accomplishments increased my optimism that I would be given a release date at my next parole hearing.

When I returned before the Board in 1994, my hopes were sky high. I was so optimistic that I called my friends and family to tell them I had a strong feeling that I'd be coming home. My brother would visit me while I was at CMC and sometimes bring his young daughter, Kesha. Those visits helped me to feel close to my family again and made my eagerness to reconnect with them outside all the more powerful. As my hopes went up, so did theirs. Once again, I was crushed. After denying my parole for another year, the Board assured me that I was on the right path. In 1995, buoyed by a similar if fragile hopefulness, I heard the same story. The depth of my despair as the years passed by—1992, 1994, 1995—the utter feeling of discouragement, was indescribable. And yet, ultimately, I was also aware that I had no one but myself to blame for my incarceration. Unfortunately, loneliness and guilt can be debilitating to any mind. That burden of guilt didn't ease with my accomplishments or other tangible evidence of an outwardly changed life. Instead, I was discovering that the ability to persevere under extremely adverse conditions with no clear end in sight was itself a powerful achievement: a testament to human resilience—a blessing from our DNA—and I needed every bit of it.

Chapter Seven

In God's Time

After being denied yet again by the Parole Board, I was on the verge of losing faith in my ability to cope. However, I was presented with an unexpected opportunity. I'd been working as an assistant in a data processing (DP) class at CMC. The instructor called me into his office, sat me down, and, sensing my anxiety, immediately said that my former X-ray instructor was aware of a position as an inmate X-ray technician at San Quentin. He said that out of all the students who graduated from his class, the instructor had thought of me first. I felt honored but told him that I wasn't interested in returning to San Quentin. My first experience there was one I was still trying to forget.

"Don't be too quick to discount the offer," he said. "X-ray technicians are in demand on the outside." Fat chance, I thought bitterly, wondering if I would ever be released from prison. He also said that this would be a valuable experience in learning how to deal with inmates who needed compassion. "As a fellow inmate," he said, "you would be uniquely qualified to relate to them."

I would never have heard this kind of talk from a guard or prison staff—and certainly never a word about compassion. Because this was an educator working for the state prison system but not in the system, he was free of numerous prison system prejudices and better able to maintain his humanity and treat inmates fairly. He naturally thought that if an inmate needed medical attention, support and care from another inmate could be comforting. I was still reluctant—but intrigued.

So I called my old X-ray instructor from my DP instructor's office and asked him if I could have a night to sleep on the decision. He said he couldn't promise that the job would still be available the next day, but he wouldn't offer it to anyone else until he heard back from me. I started to imagine working in the San Quentin hospital giving the best possible treatment to guys who weren't used to being treated with compassion and respect. I talked with a few inmates that night and they insisted that there was nothing to think about, that I had to take the job. I spoke with my cellmate at length and he agreed I should take it. He said I was the best cellmate he'd had in his ten years of prison life—probably because I never stole from him or started an argument—and that he would miss me but wished me luck. The next morning, I went into my DP instructor's office and asked one more time for his opinion. Like everyone else, he said I should take advantage of this rare opportunity to do some real work. "If things don't work out, give me call and I'll do my best to bring you back to CMC."

I called my former X-Ray instructor and asked if the job was still available. "Yes," he said. So, back I went to San Quentin State Prison in 1995 to be an X-ray technician there.

As soon as I arrived, I noticed that the feel of the main-line had changed. The smell of violence that I had become accustomed to during my first stint at San Quentin was missing. The cell blocks weren't quite as noisy. There seemed to be a new spirit at work in these infamous old tiers. My cellmate was a young man from Oakland, a manly guy with a cocky but friendly attitude, and a matter-of-fact way of communicating. I'd seen such kids many times in prison; now in my thirties, I could call them that. They grow up wary of others, having developed psychological defenses while finding their way through juvenile and adult correctional institutions. In prison, they fine-tune their style to protect themselves and be less of a target for predators, believing that most older prisoners want to use, control, or harm them in some way. Some project toughness and a no-nonsense attitude to leave no room for misunderstanding. Others alter their personality to seem withdrawn, antisocial, or even somewhat crazy, a way to keep people at a distance. Fortunately, some of these young toughs become more comfortable interacting with others after logging some prison time, adapting to the culture and finding a place in it.

After I unpacked my three bags—all of my worldly possessions—we both sat down on the bottom bunk and he pulled out his photo album. This is how it generally goes in prison culture when a new cellmate arrives: a feeling-out process before it feels okay and safe to go to sleep. We talked through most of the night. He showed me pictures of his girlfriends and I choked up inside as he spoke about how he missed his twin daughters. He pointed out how their noses looked just like his and that big noses were a trait that ran through his family.

Toward the end of our lengthy conversation he explained the next day's schedule—also a necessary part of the talk, because there may not be enough time in the morning to cover it. He said the guards sound wake-up around 6:15 and that I should immediately wash up and get ready for breakfast. The dining hall was still segregated by race and most Blacks sat against the wall on the right side of the hall. He said he usually sat with a group of guys from Oakland and I instinctively knew to tell him that I would probably sit with some people I already knew. This reduced whatever social pressure there might have been to sit with the person you "cell" with.

In the morning, I waited in bed until my cellmate finished up at the sink; only one person at a time can move around in the cell because it is very small. He then sat on his bunk and seemed to be meditating. Another fifteen minutes went by and the loudspeaker announced wake-up. The guards started releasing inmates, beginning at the top tier and working their way down; sometimes they start at the bottom tier and work their way up. Half a tier is released at one time. I washed up, got dressed, and headed to breakfast. When I got there, I saw a homeboy of mine who used to live in Chicago before getting arrested and convicted in Los Angeles for a crime he says he didn't commit. His name was Rahman and we'd met at CMC about five years ago.

He was sitting in the "Muslim section" of the dining hall. The hall, just like the yard, was segregated into groups by gang identity, geographical origin, religious interest, or non-affiliated. It wasn't safe to sit in an area that wasn't yours. I hesitated but considering how forgiving religious groups are supposed to be, I thought it least likely to cause a stir if I sat in a clearly religious area. Rahman invited me to sit down and then said he'd be working in the infirmary. I told him I'd be there as well to work in the X-ray department. He was genuinely delighted, and we walked there together. My first day as an inmate X-Ray technician at San Quentin State Prison had begun with some promise.

I performed my duties to the best of my ability and soon became obsessed with making the X-ray department a high-functioning part of the infirmary. I took X-rays of Reception Center inmates (those who had just arrived), general population inmates, and Death Row inmates. I'll never forget an afternoon when I heard loud footsteps approaching the X-ray department. I could hear the rattling of shackles and keys. Lead by a sergeant and two escorting officers, Stanley "Tookie" Williams was being brought in for an X-ray. He was on death row and infamously known as the co-founder of the L.A. Crips gang. He was a very big fellow with arms bigger than my head. His chest seemed enormous. I was standing there in the X-ray department in my smock and radiation badge on my collar looking very official. The sergeant asked me if I needed them to take the chains off of Tookie in order to perform the X-rays. Tookie looked at me as if he was trying to process where he remembered me from and it came to him almost immediately; the time I was on the terrible death row isolation unit nearly a decade earlier. He asked me how did this happen—how did I go from being on that yard to now having a sergeant ask me if it was alright to take the chains off of him. I remember that moment, but in that moment, I had no answer. I did say that I needed the chains removed off Big Tookie in order to perform the X-ray. The chains were removed!

I probably X-rayed everyone in the prison at one time or another and, in the process, became quite well-known among both inmates and staff. This was especially true during the month of tuberculosis (TB) testing, when I would spend sixteen hours a day, every day, taking X-rays. Prison administrators feared TB, not because of how it might affect inmates but because it could spread to staff. They made it mandatory for everyone at the prison.

Two days after a needle insertion test, medical staff would examine puncture marks to determine from the diameter of the mark if an inmate might have TB. If it was a certain size, he would be sent to my department for chest

X-rays. If someone did have TB, the medical staff would quarantine him, gather information about where he'd been and the people he had come in contact with, and ship him to a hospital.

After I'd returned to San Quentin, inmates from the Protestant church tried to enroll me in their programs. I felt complimented that they thought I'd be open to such pursuits—a positive reflection on my character?—but my answer was always the same: "Thanks but I'm just too busy." One Christian-based program called Kairos kept getting mentioned. Kairos is a Greek word that means "In God's Time." When I first heard that, I remember thinking about the old television commercial: "We will serve no wine before its time." It was explained to me that Kairos was designed to prepare inmates to be men of God and upstanding citizens upon their release. It had become apparent to me that if people are treated well, they tend to treat others well, and so the idea of wanting the best for others was appealing, as well as the fact that Kairos was staffed by volunteers. Still, I remained reluctant. This world is segregated by race and faith and I didn't want to join a program I feared would separate me from people of other faiths. In prison, for reasons of safety and social comfort, nearly everyone aligns with those most like them, making prisons one of the most segregated places in society—along with religious houses of worship. I had committed myself to interacting with everyone without barriers, reinforced by my work as an X-ray technician. Over the next several months, though, Christian inmates kept telling me what a life-changing experience Kairos had been for them. As I saw the impact it had on some pretty tough guys, I became increasingly curious. Finally, in October 1995, I submitted an application to the Reverend and was approved to take the next three-day workshop.

My first day attending Kairos was indeed transforming. The people who presented the program didn't seem special in any way on the surface, but they did incredible work. They didn't judge us, look down on us, or pity us. They treated us with compassion and dignity, like fellow human beings, as though we each had inherent worth. They shared stories of their lives and difficulties they had overcome. They spoke of their strong faith and commitment to helping others. I hadn't experienced anything close to this kind of treatment in my previous twelve years of incarceration.

On the second night, at the foot-washing ceremony, I had a direct experience of transcendent wonder that moved me to a renewal of spirit and an openness to the forces that create and sustain life. In San Quentin State Prison, where, in the name of the People of the State of California, fellow human beings were being put to death, I discovered my spiritual self.

Chairs and pans were set up at the front of the church. The facilitators instructed us to form two lines, which ran about twenty deep. As I inched closer and closer to the front, I struggled with my emotions and self-esteem. Did I really want to do this? It seemed so . . . different. And maybe more to the point of my anxiety: Was I worthy enough for someone to kneel down in front of me and wash my feet? When I got to the front, I stood before a tall, priestly-looking man whose gentleness helped put me at ease. When he took off my shoes and socks and placed water on my feet, I never felt so human. Inexplicably, I understood immediately that everyone is worthy of being treated with dignity. If a stranger could treat a convicted murderer the same as he might anyone else, then how could I act any less decently toward others? I was overcome with joy and gratitude for this understanding that we are all worthy of love and respect.

To say that the experience opened my eyes to a new perspective on life is not an overstatement; it literally changed the course of mine. The Kairos weekend also introduced me to a couple of men who would become life-long mentors and loving friends, seeing me through the challenges to come and never once turning away. The man who bathed my feet was John Kelly, a former priest and a long-time volunteer for Kairos. He had a remarkably deep voice and when he spoke, the walls seemed to echo his words. Eugene R. Kirkham was a former lawyer turned winery owner in California's Napa Valley. He loved helping with Kairos almost as much as he loved playing the guitar, and his life was an expression of compassion and generosity. Although his education included Harvard and Berkeley, Eugene was remarkably grounded and able to speak naturally with anyone. John and Eugene are two of the most courageous and selfless people I have ever met, ordinary men doing extraordinary things, unsung heroes of human compassion and perseverance.

Some people question if it's worth the effort trying to save inmates—even one—who have done unforgivable things. Whenever I hear this expressed I'm reminded of a story I was told—and often tell others—about the starfish. An old man was walking down the beach after a rainy night and was slowly, tirelessly bending over every few steps to pick up starfish that had washed up on shore, throwing them back into the water. A young girl walking on the beach saw the man tossing starfish into the sea and asked him why he was making such an effort to throw them back since most of them would just wash back up on shore anyway. The old man bent over, picked up another starfish, and threw it into the ocean. He looked at the little girl and gently said, "To this starfish, in this present moment, it really does matter." The girl then joined him picking up starfish and throwing them back into the ocean. To those starfish—to this starfish—it really did matter.

Many inmates noticed a change in me. I no longer considered work the only thing in life. I sought out other programs to further my personal growth. One of them was called Katargeo. Like Kairos, Katargeo is also a Greek word and basically means "letting things go." The focus of the program was to help inmates break whatever mental or attitudinal chains that were holding them back. These chains are of our own making and include such things as substance abuse and addictions, uncontrollable emotions, and persistent feelings of low or negative self-worth. Inmates involved with Katargeo learned how to forgive themselves of past mistakes and let go of inhibiting guilt.

I began practicing meditation and found the perfect place for it: the darkroom of the X-ray department. I would concentrate on my breath and then reach a point where I was no longer conscious of my body and aware only of my spirit. In my meditations, I realized that growing spiritually and being of service to my fellow human beings was much more important to me than working sixteen hours a day. I realized that having a college degree and a medical license paled in comparison to the impact I could have on someone's life by interacting with them on a personal and compassionate level. I was just as busy as ever now, but it wasn't working for the State. I was doing the work that humans were designed for: being of service in some way to others.

People used to say that I smiled all the time, but now my smile was about much more than how I felt personally. It reflected my passion for making a difference in the lives of others.

I was soon introduced to the Alternatives to Violence Project (AVP), a program that was started in the 1970s after a group of prisoners at Green Haven Correctional Facility in New York City asked Quakers to come in and speak to them about nonviolence. The program spread from there across the country. In California, a group of volunteers came into prisons and put on three-day interactive AVP workshops offering Basic and Advanced training as well as Training for Facilitators. I took the three-day Basic Workshop and was hooked. The sense of community-building; the recognition that all of us have elements of goodness and violence that affect our lives in subtle and profound ways; and the fundamental belief that everyone has the power of peace and the ability to transform violence; all spoke to the very core of my being. In 1996, after completing all the AVP training, I began to facilitate workshops. I was so happy to share the light I'd been introduced to with others. I came to rely on what I had learned and what I was teaching to keep transforming my own life—and I kept returning to the principles and teachings of Kairos, Katargeo, and AVP to get through the despair and loneliness that often still lay in wait for me.

An old inmate philosopher, Wizard, used to say about Time: "It does seem as though the weeks, months, and years constantly, repetitively, and daily creep by with the pace of a three-legged, one-eyed, three-hundred-pound turtle." Wizard's words may have felt accurate to me once, but I've since learned that time is dualistic—it can crawl by or it can fly. When we are enjoying the moment, it seems as though there is never enough time, and that gradually became my experience of it. I discovered that "doing my time" could include doing something I enjoyed, something that would impact others in a positive way. Having been blown open by Kairos and Katargeo and AVP, I found I was happiest when being of service to others. The appreciation they expressed never failed to gratify me and so, in 1997, I decided to start informal self-help groups that provided tutoring services for inmates pursuing educational degrees and certifications. We would meet on the recreation yard or in the housing units and inmates heard about us through word of mouth. Soon, there were groups for math, reading, and even guidance in preparing resumes.

The popularity of these groups made me realize how thirsty inmates were for this kind of support and so we decided to start an official "inmate activity group" that would need permission at every level of the administration all the way up to the warden. Remarkably we got it, and after the warden signed off on our request, I officially co-founded Project REACH, which stood for Reach for Education, Achievement, and Change with Help. We were assigned a staff sponsor to act as our liaison with prison officials, and the response from inmates was overwhelming. At times, we didn't have enough room or tutors to accommodate the demand. With the official sanction of the warden, inmate tutors were able to meet with inmate students at the prison library and in classrooms. Project REACH also became self-sufficient. With permission from the warden, we held fundraisers to purchase our own teaching supplies. Through our staff sponsor, we contacted local vendors and purchased discounted products that we would re-sell to inmates; the accounting office would remove the necessary funds from their accounts.

I was scheduled for another parole board hearing in early 1998, and this time I had little expectation that the result would be any different than before. And I was right. The members complimented me on the fine job I was doing, said I was getting closer, and told me to keep up the good work. Empty, easy words, especially when I knew my next hearing would be another two years away. I was beginning to understand that the entire process of standing before the Board was a sham, a game. Board members had no intention of ever recommending people for parole until they had served most if not all of their mandated time. Even then, the chances were low. Inmates usually ended up serving much more time than originally meted out by the courts. Their pleas for lenience fell on deaf ears; their good deeds and transformations were ignored; they had no voice that anyone cared to listen to. The attitude of parole boards, politicians, and police was only about being "tough on crime."

Nevertheless, I had to keep going. I continued to help inmates who came to my programs and I was always moved by positive results. It's a testament to human resilience when we realize—as I had—that it's not the mistakes we make that really matter, but how well we recover and learn from them and hopefully find some way to balm the hurts we caused.

This simple truth became as evident to me in small things as it was in the largest issues. I saw many men tormented by guilt and shame for what they had done, unable to forgive themselves and stuck in self-hatred, eager to criticize themselves or others. Their lives were daily hells of their own creation, hardened by the oppression and soullessness of the prison environment. But I also saw men who had overcome those powerful forces, who became genuinely decent, present and helpful human beings. Even small things like overcoming embarrassment can be an opportunity for growth. I had students who struggled with math problems and immediately faulted themselves for their stupidity or ignorance. Working with them, I could help soften and transform that negative energy into focus until understanding blossomed. For me these occasions were unfailingly joyous.

One student in particular, a skinny, youthful-looking, forty-something guy from San Francisco named Earnest, approached me one day outside the education building and said he wanted to speak in private. He told me he wanted to learn how to read. He had always gotten along by guessing at signs and asking questions. I told him that if he committed to our program, he'd be able to read at a sufficient level to take his GED (General Education Development) or high school equivalency exam. He said he was embarrassed to be so old and unable to read. "We have other guys your age in our program," I said. "No one will notice." He wasn't swayed and requested that I tutor him privately. I agreed but with a caveat—that he would join the other men when he felt more comfortable and prior to taking his GED. "Deal," he said, and I became his private—and discreet—

tutor. I still remember the look in Earnest's eyes when he was told, after just six months of study and practice, that he had passed his GED. Earnest was a serious and humble man who just wanted to be able to write his grandson a birthday card. It was a huge achievement for him and he thanked me profusely. I should have been the one thanking him for demonstrating the value of commitment, organization, and determination. I may have learned that in the Marine Corps but it sure felt good to see it manifested in Earnest, and in others as well.

I began to receive a lot of recognition from the staff and the correctional officers for my work in the X-ray department and with the many groups I was facilitating. I became so well-known and held in such esteem that I was chosen to introduce the warden at a banquet of dignitaries, guests, and invited inmate friends and families. The event was organized by SQUIRES—San Quentin Utilization of Inmate Resources, Experiences, and Studies. The program began in 1964 and by 1998 was reported to be the oldest juvenile awareness program in the U.S. Different public agencies brought troubled youth into San Quentin, and members of SQUIRES—a multiracial group of elder inmates—would use a tough talk, "scared straight" kind of tactic to try to discourage them from a life of crime.

Unfortunately, no good deed goes unpunished, as they say. In 2000, a certain lieutenant became unhappy that I, an inmate, was receiving so much good will from staff and inmates alike. He seemed to make it his personal mission in life to remove me from San Quentin. It didn't take long for him to create a story that would ultimately put me in hand-cuffs, parade me through the prison, and banish me back to the hole.

The X-ray department was located in the infirmary on the prison's second floor and had a fantastic view across the San Francisco Bay. Some nights after my groups, I would go there to take emergency X-rays, usually of someone's hands or face as a result of a fight. After processing the X-ray film for the attending physician, I would shower off the dark-room chemicals and look at the million-dollar homes across the water while drying off. On this particular night, I heard a loud knock on the file room door. I thought it might be the doctor or an officer alerting me to another emergency X-ray that needed to be performed. I quickly wrapped a towel around myself, went through the file room, and opened the door.

The lieutenant was standing there, red-faced, and already rattling off a barrage of questions. "What are you doing up here? Who's your supervisor? Who's in charge of you right now? Where are the free staff? Why are you showering up here? What's your name?"

Seeing that he was visibly upset, I calmly said, "I am inmate X-ray technician Alexander and the officer assigned to the front door of the infirmary knows that I'm up here. I was called over to take an emergency X-ray on an inmate. I had to shower here because I handled chemicals in the dark room." He said, "You shouldn't be up here by yourself." As he spun away, I knew I had just made an enemy.

In the days and weeks that followed, I remember being advised by different correctional officers that I was being investigated. My reply was always the same: "I'm clean as a whistle." As time moved forward, the warnings became more frequent and the tone more serious. I knew that I had done nothing wrong and foolishly thought that there was nothing for me to worry about. However, in prison, if an officer wants to accuse an inmate of wrongdoing, he doesn't need to do more than simply assert that you did it. I believed I was too well—known and respected for someone to make a trumped-up charge stick. I had lulled myself into believing that I would be treated fairly because of my positive activities and influence. But this was prison, I was an inmate, and when he was ready, the lieutenant soon made his move.

I was working in the X-ray department when I heard keys clanging, which usually meant approaching officers. My first thought was that they were bringing an inmate who needed an X- ray. The officer stationed at the front door of the infirmary walked in first. He said matter-of-factly that two officers would be escorting me to the hole. I was shocked. "Why? I haven't done anything wrong!"

"Just do as they say," he said. I was cuffed and marched out of the infirmary. It seemed as if every inmate in the prison was on the upper yard of San Quentin that day when the two officers escorted me to the hole in a kind of a slow-motion horror show. I was the focus of attention, everyone wondering and speculating "Not Alexander!" or "What did he do?" I was in total disbelief that this could be happening to me, deeply embarrassed and feeling disconnected from reality. Inmates I had tutored, staff and correctional officers who had written letters of recommendation to the Board on my behalf, even the warden whom I had introduced on stage at a major function, all would be disappointed to hear that I had been thrown into the hole.

Once there I was stripped of everything and given a pair of underwear, a towel, sheets, and a blanket. I was locked into a pitch-black cell. I still didn't know why I was in the hole or how long I would be there. No one told me anything. There were no windows, so I didn't know morning from night. The only hint of time was the arrival of breakfast or dinner. Three days later, a different lieutenant brought me in handcuffs to the interview room. I sat in front of him as he looked over some papers. It took every ounce of discipline I had to not scream out, "What is going on?" So I sat silently, the only noise in the room his breathing and the shuffling of papers.

Finally, he looked at me and asked, "Why are you here?" The only thing that came out of my mouth were the muffled words, "I don't know." The lieutenant said, "You are under investigation. You were placed in Administrative Segregation because you are deemed a threat to the safety and security of this institution." Finding my tongue, I said, "But I haven't done anything. What am I accused of?"

Instead of answering, he told me to sign a document stating that he had seen me and explained my rights. He said that someone would speak with me again. I was then escorted back to my dark cell.

A couple of days later I was handcuffed and brought again to the interview room. Two investigators (correctional officers who were assigned to conduct investigations within the prison) were seated across the table from me. One of them asked, "Do you know of any other inmates having sexual relations with a staff member?"

Other? I was dumbfounded, but all I could say was, "No."

"What about in the church?" he asked.

"No!"

"We've heard about inmates having sex with volunteers who come into the prison," he continued.

"I haven't heard anything about that," I said. The other investigator shouted that I did know something because I was having sex with a female staff in the infirmary. "No, that isn't true!" I shouted back.

Back to the hole I went, hoping as the days passed that some staff member would stand up for me. But no one did; staff will not go against other staff members, no matter how unjust an action or situation. A few months later, fighting loneliness, depression and still struggling to make peace with what happened, I was transferred to Old Folsom State Prison. It was 2001. I'd now been incarcerated for 18 years.

When the bus pulled into Old Folsom State Prison, the massive structure looked like a medieval fortress to me. It was located in a town called Represa—a fitting title for a place housing such an oppressive and intimidating institution. I was placed into Cell Block 5, which many years ago was the holding area for those awaiting execution. The cells were huge, and instead of bars the doors were made of huge iron grates akin to what you'd see in a dungeon. Each time the door clanged shut, it did so with a sound of finality, as though it would never open again. I dreaded being locked in that cell. I was losing spirit and my energy level was as low as it had ever been. I felt defeated and had no motivation to do anything other than sit and sink deeper into despair.

There wasn't much to do in Old Folsom anyway; it had only a fraction of the programs that San Quentin offered, and I wasn't interested in any of them. Rehabilitation was no longer a foreign language at San Quentin as it still was in Old Folsom. In political terminology, San Quentin was the most liberal and Old Folsom the most conservative in the California prison system. If inmates even attempted to speak casually to guards, they would quickly discover what a mistake that was. The majority of guards were under the misguided belief that the inmates were unsalvageable and deserved to be treated badly. It never seemed to occur to them that most of the inmates would be released someday and their resentment and rage might be taken out on the society that condoned such treatment. Maybe they just didn't care. Their dark mojo was certainly working on me. I felt my morale, faith, and spirit dissipating with each day.

The main recreation yard of Old Folsom was small compared with San Quentin and yet it serviced twice the number of inmates. I spent as little time there as possible and began isolating myself in my cell. It was a lonely time. An inmate who knew me from San Quentin, after finding out that I was at the prison, came to the front of my cell one day and peered through the small look-in opening. His name was Donald. "James!" he called out. He saw that I didn't seem like myself and insisted that I needed to get out of that cell and do some kind of work. I told him that there were no jobs because the prison was so overcrowded. "Give me a few days," he said confidently. "I'll come up with something."

Sure enough, Donald came to my cell a few days later and told me that the guard in charge of a small yard used by the Nortenos needed a worker to clean the place up and pass out supplies. The Nortenos were a Hispanic gang from Northern California that was kept isolated from the rest of the general population. Their rivals were Hispanics from Southern California. California prisons were constantly trying to manage incidences of violence between these two groups, and yet both were heavily represented at Old Folsom—which of course made no sense other than in the twisted logic of prison administration.

The job fit my needs because I would get to work prior to yard call and would return to my cell after the yard was closed for that day. For one reason or another, the Nortenos weren't allowed on the yard often and during those times I would have the place to myself—with absolutely nothing to do. I had to look busy because the guard was afraid that someone from admin would come through and find me idle, so we decided that I would repeatedly sweep one small section of concrete. It was obviously just busy work, but the monotony became like a meditation to me. I would grab my broom and with full concentration and determination keep sweeping this very small portion of cement.

Oddly revived by this routine, I wrote letters to my brother, my aunt Sybil, John Kelly, Eugene and others who had become my friends, telling them about this special zone that I regularly cleaned, day after day, month after month. I know it sounds crazy but focusing on that small piece of real estate every day was the lifeline I needed to sustain forward motion. The letters of encouragement from my family and friends were the fuel which kept the light of hope lit in my heart. I was most fortunate that some of my correspondence lasted for more than two decades. It should be said that a word or phrase of encouragement can change someone's life. I am so grateful to the people who were, and still are, in my life during those most trying of times. I am who I am because of them!

Chapter Eight

Choosing to Make
Love My Center

In 2004, I was told by the Old Folsom Classification Committee that I was to be transferred to Solano State Prison. I didn't know why and didn't care. I was so happy to be leaving Old Folsom that I went back to my cell and did jumping jacks for what seemed like hours. I had survived Old Folsom for three years with my sanity intact and a more profound understanding of myself. I now knew, beyond a shadow of a doubt, that I could withstand whatever situation or circumstance I found myself in as long as I had breath and didn't give up—mentally, spiritually, or physically. It also helped tremendously to have had the steadfast support of others. This hard-earned understanding would aid me greatly in the difficult years to come.

Solano was very different from Old Folsom. The huge dungeon cells of Folsom were replaced by dormitory-style living units without doors, crammed with inmates sleeping on bunk-beds, and stacked sometimes three levels high.

There were twelve men per room and often more. The overcrowding of the prison system had become worse as the state's conservative parole policy and aggressive enforcement of low-level drug laws stretched existing capacity to the breaking point. The additional stress on the guards was obvious as they argued more and more often with each other about who was responsible for unit tasks and assignments. Prison officials responded by hiring more guards. The guards' union applauded the increase because the dues fattened their coffers and generated salary increases and useful contributions to the re-election campaigns of favored lawmakers—a cycle that continued for years. The losers in this swollen population were, of course, the inmates.

I had never lived in a dorm before and it took patience and tolerance to function and sleep in wide-open unprotected quarters with eleven or more others. On top of that, the building held about 260 inmates, all living in similar dorm rooms with open access to any other room any time. Each dorm room policed itself with informal rules regarding such things as noise, cleaning responsibilities, and at what times the room would be off limits to other inmates. Each building was like a homeowners' association with each dorm room like a member. If someone violated a dorm rule or agreement, the consequences could range from a fight to being expelled. The guards were more lenient here than those in higher security facilities. There were more fights but fewer stabbings, shootings, and fatalities than in the powder keg prisons I'd endured over most of the last twenty years. There were, however, many more drugs.

It's a common misconception that friends and family smuggle in most drugs discovered in prisons. They are, in fact, supplied mostly by the guards in every prison I was ever in. The guards also smuggle in the majority of flip phones and (later) cell phones. The guards would select favored inmates, usually gang members, to distribute the phones and drugs. The cost for drugs and phones was high because of the risk premium. Inmates would have their contact on the outside put $700 into an account. Once the payment was verified, the inmate would get a phone. Of course, when the demand for the phones would rise, so too would the cost. No price was too high for men desperate for contact with the outside world. Guys yearned to talk to their wives, girlfriends, parents, relatives, or friends. Some inmates took their phones under their blanket at night and talked in whispered tones for hours. In buildings where the guards initiated frequent safety checks, inmates would have other inmates looking out for them. Guards often swept buildings and dorms to find and confiscate phones and drugs. Some guards profited mightily from this game. For addicted inmates, the phone was a short-term benefit followed by an accumulation of penalties and suffering.

I chose to not play. Inmates who were friendly toward me sometimes offered the use of their phones, but I always declined because the risks were too great. I knew how quickly things could go bad in prison and I wanted to stay clear of any traps. I used the legal prison phone once a week, a time-consuming process but much safer. You had to stand in a long line the night before the call and schedule both the phone (there was more than one) and the time you wanted to use it. Each call lasted exactly 15 minutes. The prison profited on these calls because the phone carrier charged high rates to the inmate's family and friends and the prison got a kickback from the carrier. If something happened during the appointed hour and you missed your call, you would have to repeat the entire procedure again. But, like everything else in prison life you get used to it.

I started participating in productive activities again and cleansing myself of the darkness of Old Folsom. Eugene's former wife, Cody, visited me regularly at Solano. I had met Eugene during the Kairos weekend in San Quentin back in 1995. He and Cody had remained in touch with me since then. Cody would show up once a month and brave the long and humiliating treatment family and friends of inmates have to endure to enter the prison, from filling out numerous forms to undergoing physical searches. I believe the process is designed to be demeaning and time-consuming to dissuade people from visiting. However, Cody, like many friends and family of inmates, braved the degradation to bring the light of love into the prison. I often told her how much I admired her courage.

I began inviting other inmates to sit in informal groups with me to discuss different topics. The spirit was educational and our conversations covered a lot of ground. We even formed a stock market group, selecting and following stocks on the Dow. We weren't using real money, of course, but for inmates who had never read the financial section of a newspaper, the process gave them a feel for the real world in a way they'd never experienced. Now that I was helping others again, my optimism was returning and I was feeling once again that my life had a purpose. I regained my confidence that I could be a contributing member of society and re-committed myself to getting a parole release date.

Even though my record of accomplishments continued to gain additions, I was still being denied parole by the California Board of Parole Hearings (BPH) at Old Folsom and during my first year at Solano. During that difficult time, the communities of Kairos and Alternatives to Violence Project, along with my network of friends and family, kept stepping up, writing letters and working tirelessly to convince the Board of my suitability for release. I was amazed and inspired by their perseverance. My Kairos brother, fellow AVPer, and dear friend Eugene Kirkham, had even renewed his California attorney's license to represent me before the Board in 2006. So I was hopeful once again.

There are three phases to California Parole Board hearings. In the first phase, the Board looks at your record and questions you about the crime. The best I could hope for during that phase was to maintain some composure when they spoke of my murder conviction.

In the second phase, the Board investigates your prison record and examines everything you have done while in prison—the good, bad, and indifferent. It's during this phase, if you've done well, that you can begin to hold your head a little higher and raise your eye level.

In the third and final phase, the Board questions your plans for the future after your release. This is when (at least in theory) your hopes begin to rise as you focus on your life ahead as a free man.

By this time in the proceedings, however, most inmates are so beaten down by the process, their re-telling of the original crime, and long recitals of their prison history, that they have obliterated all hope of success. Instead of a strong finish stating why they should be granted parole, they have reserved barely enough energy to convince anyone that they would do well outside prison walls. Before this final chance to make their case, a good attorney will try to help an inmate refocus and recover after the needling and dissection of the Parole Board. In a very narrow window, the attorney must rebuild the inmate's self-esteem and convince them to keep the faith that their effort will make the difference in transforming their future. It's a skill that many state-appointed attorneys never develop because it requires practice, time, and dedication from these underpaid (and often unmotivated) "public servants." A passion for justice also helps.

Eugene was not a state-appointed attorney or a private attorney out for the money. He was a friend who cared about my welfare and was motivated by the injustice of my situation. After Eugene gathered and organized all the information available, he made a powerful and effective case for my release. The Board, chaired by a conservative, white, male, former District Attorney from Humboldt County, listened and then went into their deliberations. The guards escorted me back to the cage where other inmates awaited their hearing. The inmates bombarded me with questions:

"Who are the Board members?"

"Are they tough?"

"Do you think you got a shot?"

The questions usually go on until it's time for the guard to escort the prisoner who's up next into the hearing room.

During the 1980s, the Parole Board panel had three members. But in the 90s and 2000s, a growing backlog of hearings forced the board to reduce the number to two, a Commissioner who was appointed by the Governor and a Deputy Commissioner who was a bureaucrat with law enforcement background, in hopes of speeding up the process. Governor-appointed Board members routinely turned down inmate requests for parole because when they didn't, the Governor usually overruled their decision. Displeasing the Governor meant the real possibility of losing their appointment or not being reappointed if they granted too many paroles. In the rare event of a split decision, the case would be referred to the nine Commissioners of the full Board in what was called an en banc hearing where a final decision would be made.

Eugene came back to the cage to speak to me. Since there was no attorney-client privacy in front of the cage, he requested and received permission to take me into the interview room. It was being used by another attorney so we waited outside in the corridor, pacing up and down the hall. My mind was filled with thoughts of our friends, family, and supporters who had dedicated so much energy and prayed so long for a positive outcome. I couldn't bear to see them disappointed again. Eugene did all he could to lighten up the moment, helping me focus on the possibility of a life enriched by service to others. But when you're waiting on a life-changing decision over which you have no control, moments feel very heavy indeed and seem like days.

We were startled by the loud clank of the gate. It was the guard motioning us to return to the hearing room. I seized up with fear. My legs became cement and my breath shortened. I could not speak, and my eyes blurred. I was literally holding onto Eugene as we made our way back. I sat down at the large desk feeling the vast gulf between us and the Commissioners. As I reflect back on that scene and mindful of the irony, I believed then and still believe that no human being should ever wield that kind of life-and-death power over another.

Then the Chairman spoke. I was so numb I could barely hear what he was saying. "You have presented a strong case of rehabilitation and suitability for release and we grant your petition for parole." Just like that. I was stunned, wondering if I had heard him correctly. Could it really be true that after twenty-three years, my time in prison was finally coming to an end? I turned to Eugene and saw the delighted look on his face. I realized it must be true and a massive weight lifted off my heart and my tears began to flow. The tireless efforts of Eugene and all the others who had supported my release had finally paid off. My heart soared like an eagle.

We of course told everyone the news at the first opportunity—family, inmates and outside friends—and their euphoria was palpable. Then the unthinkable happened. In June of 2006, five months after the Board Panel ruled in my favor, the Honorable Governor Arnold Schwarzenegger (who at the time, as reported later, was having an affair with his maid) overruled the Board's decision.

Despite having my parole denied many times, I had never been granted an actual release date before. To have it reversed was crueler than any punishment the State could devise—like saving a man's life just so you could execute him. I knew the impact this would have on my family and friends. We had never been so close to freedom before. To their credit, though, they remained steadfast in their support. Without that community of people buoying me up, I'm not sure I could have gone on.

I continued teaching my classes and facilitating the AVP workshops. I had no choice, and the work of helping others kept my own spirit from crashing into depression. At least I had my work to do.

The following year my advocate Eugene was at my side again when I returned to the California BPH. A new chairperson heard our case—and again stated that I was a great example of rehabilitation and suitable for release! During the next five months, my family and friends prepared for my homecoming. I was careful to warn them—and myself—not to be too hopeful. But even in the face of past experience, expectation can be dangerously seductive. Five months after the second Board's second decision to set me free, Governor Schwarzenegger once again readjusted the famous blindfold of justice and reversed the Board again.

A painful blow—but I knew from experience that I would get through it. I was more concerned for the spirits and stamina of my family and friends. This second blow would test even the most loyal heart. To his enormous credit, Eugene didn't drop a stitch. He helped to keep the resolve of my family and friends rock solid.

I returned to teaching classes, facilitating workshops, and offering a patient audience to anyone who needed it. My work in healing others was becoming more and more central, giving my life meaning and purpose, even in prison. "Maybe I'm only meant to accomplish what I can do from inside prison," I would think. "Maybe I will never leave these four walls." Maybe a life of service, and not necessarily freedom, should be my goal.

But in 2008, as my next hearing date drew near, the familiar anxiety returned—the mixture of fear and hope. One definition of insanity is repeating the same action over and over again and expecting a different result; but in this case, there was no choice. So there I was, back before the Board again. After the usual round of queries and reports from the record, the new woman chairperson stated, "I've had the opportunity to sit across from you, look you in the eye, and have a conversation with you today. I think other people should have that opportunity too. You are thirteen years overdue for parole." She paused for emphasis, saw the expression on my face, and continued. "That's right. You should have been released thirteen years ago. I hope the people who review today's record really hear what I'm saying."

How could I not feel confident? Other inmates were equally certain. They would tell me things like, "This is the last summer you'll see the inside of this place!" or "You won't be eating this mush much longer" or "Won't it be nice to take a shower by yourself?"

I'd spent a lot of time with these guys and whatever their circumstances, most of them cheered when someone got out. I was in constant contact with family and friends by mail and phone and visits. Four months, three weeks, and five days went by. Then six days…I was assured by the jailhouse lawyers that it was illegal for the Governor to reverse a decision after the five-month review period. And this time, his time was up.

But the people who make the rules don't have to follow them. Two days later—five months and three days after the Board decided I was suitable for release for the third time—Governor Schwarzenegger again reversed their decision.

The "tough on crime/blind to justice" ideology that dominated state politics was firmly cemented in place.

Accompanying this third rejection came a compounding cruelty that pushed me to the edge. It was as if some mysterious Machiavellian mechanism was specifically focused on destroying my mind. A new state initiative had just passed, increasing the wait time between parole hearings from one year to three. Now the Governor would not exhaust himself saying no each year; he would only have to utter it every three years. My mind refused to grasp the terror of this new law. Another three years before I could plead for my freedom again—to be stuck in limbo until 2011 with no chance of release despite three affirmative hearings by the Parole Board was a type of oppressive torture I could not bear.

Even more terrifying, this new law increased the *maximum* waiting period between hearings to fifteen years, if the Board chose. So, for example, if a young gang member started a fight with a "term-to-life" inmate (someone like me who had to appear before the Board to get released from prison), both would be disciplined for violating regulations. The gang member would receive maybe an extra 90 days on his sentence. The Board, empowered by its new rules, could—and likely would—impose the maximum waiting period on the older (victimized) inmate—fifteen years.

Imagine if a guard had it in for a particular inmate. It would be easy to arrange such an attack. This could have happened to me had the law been in place back when I was falsely accused of sexual relations with a female prison staff member at San Quentin. And I knew it could happen again.

In prison, there is nowhere to run and hide. Every day an inmate wakes up and has to face whatever confronts him, ready or not. Some prisoners, when they can no longer stand the abuse, uncertainty, or depression, choose the only other available option—escape by taking their own life. After this latest turn of the screw, the idea did not seem so terrible. The screams inside my head were as loud as they had been in the San Quentin hole twenty years before. I cried out to my closest friends on the outside that I was at the end of my rope.

For most of my time inside, I had been a rock, but now that rock was crumbling. Most of my friends were older and had grandchildren. They had their own lives that required attention. Yet, they assured me again that they would help me shoulder my burden. Their encouragement was a life raft but my resolve to survive was weakening.

John Kelly of Kairos, the former priest who had once blown my mind by washing my feet, visited me at Solano and asked me what would lift my spirits. I had no answer for him. He began talking about the things that had always motivated me previously—helping others, especially with their education. He asked if I was willing to accept help to further my own education. "Yes," I responded, wondering how that could possibly happen.

John then spoke with Pat Tubman, a long-time volunteer at San Quentin who was very much loved and respected by the inmates. She came to the prison once a week to facilitate a religious group meeting and was also one of the women who cooked for the Kairos men during the three-day workshop. Pat and her husband, David, agreed to underwrite the entire cost for me to pursue a bachelor's degree in psychology. Their offer and obvious care and concern snapped me out of my funk. I immersed myself in my studies, using the light from the toilet area at 1:00 a.m. because it was the quietest time in the building. I remember receiving my first "A" and saying to myself, "If I can get one "A," then I can get another." Three years later, I finished with all "A's" and a bachelor's degree in Psychology, Summa Cum Laude.

During the three years after the governor's third reversal, I also had the opportunity to participate in a pilot program designed to train inmates as drug and alcohol abuse counselors. A group of fifty inmates were selected from thousands of applications submitted. The best professionals in the field of addiction therapy and recovery were brought in to teach us therapeutic models and techniques for working with those struggling with substance abuse issues. It was at this time that I met a brilliant psychiatrist named Sol Weingarten, who taught us about the parallel process of learning about ourselves while helping others. He captured our attention immediately when he asked if we wanted to have better relations with our friends and families, and everyone we met. Who wouldn't say yes to that?

Dr. Weingarten stood out because of his ability to suspend judgment and criticism; he seemed to genuinely care about helping us to become better people. He shared his knowledge of the human mind and human behavior and was able to convey highly technical information about the workings of the brain, especially the amygdala, which has a great deal of power over our emotions. He demonstrated how to improve our interactions with friends and family and how to ask them for help and support in a way that respected their own needs. Dr. Weingarten, whom I remain in contact with to this day, has dedicated his life to teaching others—many of them inmates—how to operate from a higher level of consciousness. Working with his tools, I came to believe more strongly than ever that anyone, no matter how far they've fallen, can transform themselves into a good and decent person.

My dear friend and attorney, Eugene was enraged by this third reversal by the governor. "Enough is enough!" he said. He filed papers with the Superior Court of California claiming that an injustice had taken place which required the Court's remedy. The Superior Court Judge agreed and, after months of back and forth filings between Eugene and the Attorney General's office, the Court ordered my immediate release. The judge found that the Governor's reversal of the Parole Board's decision was not based on any evidence of my being a current threat to society.

My spirits started to lift but the battle had not yet been won. Governor Schwarzenegger, playing out his on-screen reputation as a bad-ass "terminator," requested and received an immediate Stay of the Superior Court's Order. The matter now rested in the hands of the State Court of Appeal. However, since the law increasing the wait time for parole re-consideration had not yet taken effect and another year had passed, I received another hearing date.

By this time, the Board included a man with a well-deserved reputation as one of the worst bureaucrats in the state. A divorced alcoholic who had lost his family, he was angry at life and seemed to hate his job. This particular official was reported to have never found a single prisoner suitable for release. "Maybe we should postpone the hearing and wait for another board panel," I suggested to Eugene.

"You don't know what the next one will be like," he responded, "and if it goes south you may not get another chance for three years, or more." I heard him! I was also aware that many people had been supporting me and were eager to see me released. It didn't seem fair to anyone including myself to not keep fighting.

As usual, Eugene and I were well-prepared when we entered the hearing room, buoyed by the fact that the previous three hearings had all found me suitable for parole and that the Superior Court had actually ordered my immediate release. Furthermore, I had continued to excel in all my endeavors inside the prison. The Board had ample evidence that I was not a threat to society. But to some, facts are simply obstacles en route to a pre-ordained destination.

During the new hearing, the Deputy Commissioner with the bad rep repeatedly alluded to inaccuracies in the record. He knew full well that they had been corrected before my first hearing, but he still dedicated an inordinate amount of time to issues that had been thoroughly and previously addressed. His tactics appeared to be motivated by an implacable hostility towards me that was visible to all.

The hearing lasted an unusually long five hours. The deliberation was long as well. The Commissioner spoke first. "In my opinion, you are suitable for release on parole." She then took some time describing how I had done everything humanly possible to show I was remorseful for my crime and had taken full advantage of every opportunity to further my rehabilitation. But while she was in favor of my release, the hostile Deputy Commissioner was not. A split decision meant that the case would now go to the full board of nine commissioners for an "en banc" (full court) hearing. In accordance with the rules, I would not be allowed to be present at that hearing.

My community of supporters met in Sacramento where the hearing was to be held and organized what they described to me as a "spiritual" gathering. While I listened on a prison phone, Peter Yarrow (of Peter, Paul, and Mary), led the group in the song, "The Day Is Done." I was sobbing as I listened to their voices, filled with gratitude that they had all come together on my behalf. Most were members of

Kairos, sharing their love of fellow humans with those in prison who desperately needed some positive experience of self-worth. Eugene was the glue holding this remarkable collection of people together. They were optimistically confident that their voices would be heard and that the full board would again find me suitable for parole.

At the hearing, my friends and family members—including my mother, my brother and his wife and family—offered testimony about what I had made of my life in prison and the positive impact I'd had on others. Eugene and several other attorneys spoke of the Superior Court's decision and the three prior BPH decisions which had found me suitable for parole.

In response, the District Attorney's representative, buoyed by the Governor's three reversals and the Deputy Commissioner's stance, spoke at length about the original crime, the stabbing assault more than twenty years earlier in Soledad, and the trumped-up charge of sexual relations with a female staff member in San Quentin in 2000. The Deputy Commissioner's testimony made the issue personal, suggesting that his years of service to the state should count for something. Incredibly, the full Board voted unanimously to deny my parole.

My supporters were shocked, in disbelief, their faith in justice—tenuous after so many rebuffs—shaken to its core. When I heard the news, I was of course stunned, especially because there had been no new or negative evidence entered. The Board's decision made it quite clear that it was operating on principles other than justice. The final nail in this new coffin was that the California Court of Appeals reversed the Superior Court's decision ordering my immediate release. Every avenue had been bricked over, closed into a dead end.

I was now in my twenty-fifth year of incarceration. But instead of sinking into despair, I somehow came to terms with the reality of my situation. I couldn't control the actions of the Governor or the Board; the only thing I could control was my response. Though at first it was painful, I chose to continue my service in the prison and to continue inspiring my supporters to keep going. I circulated a message assuring everyone that justice would ultimately be served, however long it might take.

I didn't really believe it myself, but I had no choice. I simply had to be resilient. I had known depression and its debilitating effects intimately, and I didn't want to return to that wasteland ever again. I also was determined not to allow Schwarzenegger or his minions to destroy my spirit. But despite all resolve and best intentions, there are limits to what a human being can tolerate, and I was facing that limit.

Eugene, my family, friends, and supporters pooled their resources. They researched and then hired the best attorney in the state to represent me, one experienced in matters of parole, the courts, and the Governor's office.

When I first met Michael Satris, the new attorney, I was struck by his movie star charisma. He appeared to be rich, smart, full of vigor, and in possession of a full head of blind-ingly white hair. The problem was, he was expensive—and I didn't really like him. Michael was bold and harsh with an aggressive side, quite unlike the people I'd been working with. He didn't seem to care about my history of injustice; he seemed to care only about legal strategy—motions, ap-peals, writs, etc. etc. I remember insisting to Eugene that I wanted him to remain as my attorney. To his credit, and to my great relief, Eugene agreed to stay on and function as a second chair. Meanwhile he urged me to trust Satris and keep my misgivings to myself.

Michael, whom I later discovered was co-founder of the highly-respected Prison Law Office in Berkeley, hit the ground running. He filed papers in the federal courts, state courts, and with the California Board of Parole Hearings. Just as quickly, both the BPH and federal court summarily denied his filings and the new petition.

It seemed to me that we could have achieved similar re-sults on our own and I began questioning why this new at-torney was so expensive. I decided to schedule a call on the inmate phone list and tell him my concerns. I even practiced what I was going to say, wanting to explain my disappoint-ment without sounding like an ingrate. But before I had that chance, I was called to the counselor's office, where I was put on the phone with my attorney. A special call! Michael Satris told me that the Superior Court had ordered more fact-find-ing and ordered the District Attorney to submit more documentation. He assured me that this was a positive development and allayed some of my anxiety.

Months passed, and my routine remained the same. My satisfying work as a teacher and drug counselor kept depression at bay, and I tried to keep a low profile otherwise. But in the daily course of prison life there is always something to avoid or watch out for. And after more than two decades of incarceration, I'd become very adept at recognizing potentially hazardous situations—a foresight I wish I'd developed earlier in life.

One place where situations flared up regularly was the chow hall. Inmates are herded there twice a day and fights break out with little provocation. The slightest glance, a whiff of disrespect, or an accidental bump is enough to unleash someone's demons. I knew that if I could avoid the chow hall, the danger of being involved in an unwanted drama—jeopardizing my chance at parole—would substantially decrease. I had to figure out how to make myself scarce. And who came to my rescue? Eugene.

I explained the situation and humbly asked him for a stipend of one hundred dollars a month, so I could buy my own food and prepare my own meals. He generously agreed, and it affectionately became known as my "tuna allowance." I would call Eugene on the inmate telephone on Sunday evenings, usually when he and his family were sitting down for dinner. I would always apologize for interrupting his meal and explain that it was the only time available on the phone list. Invariably, either Eugene, his wife (Katrina), or his son (Liam) would ask if I was having tuna for dinner. It was an inside joke because they knew I ate tuna every night. Yes, every night! But it was still better than what they served in the chow hall. I developed hundreds of ways to prepare and eat tuna fish, happy to steer clear of the chow hall. That tuna allowance became critical to maintaining my mental health.

My situation had become one of the convicts' ongoing narratives. "Poor James," inmates would say. "Three times granted parole and still in prison." Gang leaders would use me as an example, telling their members that it didn't matter if an inmate was a "goodie two shoes;" it still wouldn't get you out of prison. Prison staff would tell me that if it was up to them, I'd be "long gone." Even some guards seemed to take pity on me, asking how I was doing or if I needed anything from the kitchen.

Time plodded on and I made my peace with it all, continuing my counseling and AVP workshops. I didn't feel bitter about the denials or the court decision. On the contrary, the love of family and friends gave me a tremendous lift and a renewed sense of courage. I decided that I would not allow my situation to define me; I would define myself by how I responded to it, and I chose to respond with love. Something deep had shifted in me. I realized that the power of the many people who loved me far outweighed the disregard of the few who extracted pleasure from my suffering. By focusing on gratitude for that love in my life, I had little room left for hate. I had love for the prisoners who teased me, for the guards who mistreated me, for the criminal justice system with its one-sided approach to justice. I chose to make love my center. This kept my attention on something greater than anything else I would ever face. People wondered why I smiled so much, how I could endure so much and still look happy. Pardon the cliché, but for me, love conquered all. After all those years I'd spent alone pondering my fate, searching for ways to deal with my depression and despair, I finally realized that I had the power to choose what I thought and felt. And I chose the feeling of love over all the others.

In 2011, Michael, Eugene, and I addressed the California Board of Parole Hearings. The Deputy Commissioner who had played a major role in extending my prison time three years before, was staring at me like a predator considering its prey. He sat directly across from me on the other side of that large table, but his stare was so penetratingly hateful that the table seemed to shrink. I felt his eyes were searching mine for a hate to match his own, a volley to return his serve—but it wasn't there.

Love was all I had left. Throughout the hearing, question after question, I responded with love. Love is what I had practiced during the previous three years, a practice that had become my way of life. I had become like a monk and the prison had become my monastery. It had changed the prisoners who disrespected or threatened me into men who spoke of me with respect. It had changed the guards' mistreatment of me into behavior that could have been interpreted as favoritism. And finally, it brought the criminal justice system to a place of compassion.

After the Board deliberated, the Deputy Commissioner gave me a very different look. "Alexander, you will be an ambassador," he said. After declaring that I was suitable for release, he got up from his chair, walked around that large table, and extended his hand. I looked at it for a moment that felt like a lifetime—then I stood up and shook it. The great peacemaker Dr. Martin Luther King Jr. once said, "Love is the only force capable of transforming an enemy to a friend." Apparently, he was onto something.

We prepared ourselves to wait the five months required for the review process to conclude. We were well aware that California had elected a new governor, Jerry Brown, who seemed to bring a different ethic of governance to the office. It was as if a ray of sunshine had slipped through the dark clouds: I gave myself permission to dream and to hope, but of course, I had traveled this road many times before. Day after day, my breathing got shorter as my anxiety rose. I wondered aloud to Eugene what would become of me if I had to endure another disappointment. I was also very concerned about all the people who had stayed with me throughout this ordeal. How could I, in good conscience, ask them to continue on such a futile and never-ending quest if once again my request was denied?

In April of 2011, less than three months after the Deputy Commissioner had walked around the table to shake my hand, the California Court of Appeals ordered my immediate release from prison. They found that Governor Schwarzenegger had abused his discretion in reversing the Board's previous decisions. The prison guards told me at four in the afternoon that I would be released at four the next morning. I had twelve hours to prepare. "That's not enough time!" I said. "I still have too much to do, too many people to say goodbye to."

"Well," they said, "you could stay another thirty years saying your goodbyes." Of course, I didn't sleep! On April 13, 2011, I was released from prison after serving twenty-eight consecutive years of incarceration.

Chapter Nine

From Hell to St. Helena

Eugene, his wife Katrina, and his ex-wife (and business partner) Cody were all waiting for me at the parole agent's office. We stepped out into the sunshine together and took pictures. I am looking at them today. In one, there is a cross behind Eugene; in another, a cross behind my head. I can see now that they were actually telephone poles—but the impression captured the magic of that incredible day.

We drove from the parole agent's office to Bosko's, a restaurant in Calistoga. After we were seated I slowly took in the beauty of the place—my first meal outside prison in nearly thirty years. Even the menu in my hands was beautiful. I ordered halibut, having told many people over the years that this is what I would order as soon as I got out. When I saw the price, I remembered I was on a tuna fish budget and was greatly relieved when Cody said I could have whatever I wanted. I did have a check for $200, issued by the state of California to every inmate when they leave prison, whether they've served six months, six years, or sixty years. I couldn't cash it, though, because at that time the prison administration wasn't allowing inmates to leave with state identification cards. So, I had a check I couldn't cash because I couldn't prove that I was Alexander!

After the wonderful meal and some great conversation, we headed for Eugene's house in St. Helena. Driving past rolling hills, vineyards, and sprawling estates, I took in through eyes like a child how truly beautiful nature is. When we arrived at Eugene's vineyard and started up the long driveway, I thought of how the prodigal son must have felt returning home and running through his father's fields. Of course, I wasn't Eugene's son and there was nothing "prodigal" about me, but my euphoria was real.

At the house, we started making phone calls to spread the news of my release. We walked outside by the pool and I noticed a small house that was being renovated and extended. My friends told me that was where I'd be staying while I was working at the winery. Eugene and Cody (his ex) have owned their winery in the Napa Valley since the late 1970's. It's called Casa Nuestra, meaning "Our House." A day or so later, Eugene and his wife threw a big party and most of my family, friends, and supporters—including my dear mother, who had waited for this moment for nearly thirty years—came to celebrate. We cried, laughed, danced, sang, and ate. I had never tasted truly good wine and Eugene's was considered among the best in Napa Valley—a far cry from Fat Joe's pruno. I was truly in a different world.

After working in the winery for a year, I was ready and able to continue my work as a counselor. With the help of many—including the mayor of St Helena—I got a job as a drug and alcohol counselor. I found that my training of working with prisoners and understanding my own journey uniquely qualified me to be non-judgmental when relating to my clients in St. Helena. I also rediscovered the peace and fulfillment I had found in listening to and helping others.

My Kairos brothers and Alternatives to Violence community continued to assist me in my journey as a returning citizen. The new friendships which I established proved very beneficial as well.

One such friendship is with Dick Grace, another Napa Valley winery owner. He has helped me tremendously in my adjustment back to life. A fellow former Marine with a "can-do" spirit, Dick invited me to join his men's group. He gave me a watch with an engraved slogan: "Be Optimystic." I thought that was very cool. I am definitely optimistic, but I'm not so sure about the mystical part. I wear the watch today.

Dick Grace also has a way with words. In introducing me to his men's group, he commented that I endured my journey through the California prison system "like a lonely monk—helping others and educating myself while suffering with deprivation and internal loneliness."

Chapter Ten

If Given a Chance . . .

As I made St. Helena my home while working for the County of Sonoma in their Department of Behavioral Health, I met all kinds of people and navigated the typical challenges and opportunities that "normal" life brings. I continued to speak before audiences and tell my story in homes, churches, and schools. People encouraged me to write a book, convinced that my story about our structural mistreatment of human beings and the resilience of the human spirit was important to share with a larger audience. I resisted at first, because I knew that my story is not unique—or shouldn't be.

Thousands of inmates suitable for release remain trapped in prison because the criminal justice system is unable—or unwilling—to facilitate actual life-affirming reforms. Most prisoners don't have the resources I had in terms of family, friends, and committed supporters, and even with all that, my process took years with numerous heart-breaking setbacks. In prison, I tutored hundreds of men and also learned their stories. Many had committed their lives to bettering themselves in the hope that one day they would be free and have the opportunity to be a constructive part of their community. I believe on the bases of 28 years of study and observation, that if given a chance, such men will have a positive impact not only on their families but on society at large. But, in order for this change to occur, they will need help.

From the mid-eighties to the 2000s, the California prison system led the world in prison construction and incarceration. During that time, the state built 23 new prisons at a cost of between $280 million to $350 million each. *To keep them filled,* conservative Parole Board commissioners were appointed, and parole was routinely denied. During these same years, the prison population increased 500% and occupancy ran at more than 190 percent.

From 1980 to 1986, the largest racial group in California prisons was Caucasian; from 1986 to 1992 it was African Americans (who made up 40% of the prison population but only 7% of the general public in California); from 1992 to the present it has been Hispanics. Coincidence?

The public portrait of prison as a gang-dominated, drug-saturated environment rings a terrible but familiar tone; staff complicity and the illegal enabling of prison guards are less widely known but central to prison's cultural violence and dysfunction. The tension created by racial divisions and separation—used by prison administrators as a method of control—add to the chaos and uncertainty.

I spent twenty-eight continuous years in the California prison system. Like every other prison system in this country, it's designed to punish and dehumanize. Inmates are encouraged to mistrust each other and live in fear, and then this is used to justify prison as the most segregated areas in our country, insuring that violence remains the usual form of "justice" and revenge. It's not as if those who end up in prison are angels or misunderstood—many will remain trapped in negative patterns of thinking and behavior—but most are victims of the environment they were raised in and of a system that does not encourage or even recognize their capacity to change.

In fairness, prison staff, from top to bottom, have a difficult job because the system is rigged to encourage conflict and mistrust. No one argues that security issues are not important or denies that tight management practices are critical to ensure the health and safety of all concerned; but the way that these concerns are executed actually create the opposite effect. Where is humanity modeled or taught?

But even in such environments—as close to hell as any war zone—human beings can still find redemption and the human spirit can still transcend and soar. I offer my own transformation as evidence, as well as the stories of inmates I worked with who also longed to create a better life for themselves and others.

All those years in prison left me with some fundamental questions: How can we make the criminal justice system more just, more effective, and less costly? How can we make it a place where positive change occurs more regularly?

My mission now is to help change the laws that exacerbate the downward spiral of human misery and to reform the prison system so that inmates are introduced to and learn to model dignity, kindness, and consideration for others; that they be given a chance through programs and classes to experience their redemptive potential.

I found my way out largely because of a handful of good-hearted volunteers from established and successful programs, who came to the prison and treated us like fellow human beings, worthy of love and respect. In less than three years after my release, I've worked as an alcohol and drug abuse counselor helping hundreds of people; I was on the Board of the California Association of Alcoholism and Drug Abuse Counselors as Regional Director representing the Napa and Sonoma Valleys; I'm on the Board of the Friend's Committee on Legislation in California (FCLCA).

I was honored by His Holiness the Dalai Lama in 2014 as an "Unsung Hero of Compassion" for all the programs I started and supported during my incarceration. Imagine that—standing on a stage in front of more than five hundred people at the Ritz Carlton Hotel in San Francisco, with many more watching the live stream over the Internet. I will never forget the moment the Dalai Lama embraced me on that stage. "Good work, my son!" he said as he looked me in the eye.

How many others who've been languishing inside our prison system are capable of doing good work in the world if given a decent chance? It's long past time to transform the way we treat those behind prison walls, whatever the crimes they committed. Their salvation will also be our own.

About the Author

James Alexander was born and raised in Chicago, served as a United States Marine, and was sentenced to prison after committing an accidental murder. He achieved certifications as an Electronic Technician, X-ray Technician, and Drug and Alcohol Abuse Counselor while in prison. James has a master's degree in Psychology and was honored as an Unsung Hero of Compassion by His Holiness, the Dalai Lama, for helping to develop self-help programs for other inmates. With *Courage in the Face of Cruelty*, he takes the reader on a remarkable journey through his 28 years in the California prison system, removing the veil of secrecy and opening the gates widely for all to see. James describes the inhumanity in simple terms and shows how inmates treat each other and how correctional officers treat inmates. He also uncovers the corrupt nature of unfair politicians who exploit human beings as fodder for their "tough on crime" stance.

Letter to My Readers

Thank you very much for reading my book, *Courage In the Face of Cruelty.*

I appreciate your interest and hope you found it as rewarding and insightful to read as it was to write.

I would so appreciate your taking a moment to write to me at jamesalexandercourage@gmail.com and let me know what you think.

If you would like, you could also write an honest review wherever you bought this book online, like Amazon. Here's a direct link to my author page on that site: amazon.com/author/jamesalexandercourage. Just click on the book cover.

Thank you very much again for reading my book.

Warm regards,

James Alexander
Jamesalexandercourage.com

Made in the USA
Lexington, KY
06 December 2019